THE ESSENTIAL KARATE BOOK

FOR WHITE BELTS, BLACK BELTS AND ALL KARATEKA IN BETWEEN

GRAEME JOHN LUND

TUTTLE Publishing

Tokyo | Rutland, Vermont | Singapore

Please note that the publisher and author of this instructional book are NOT RESPONSIBLE in any manner whatsoever for any injury that may result from practicing the techniques and/or following the instructions given within. Martial arts training can be dangerous—both to you and to others—if not practiced safely. If you're in doubt as to how to proceed or whether your practice is safe, consult with a trained martial arts teacher before beginning. Since the physical activities described herein may be too strenuous in nature for some readers, it is also essential that a physician be consulted prior to training.

Published by Tuttle Publishing, an imprint of Periplus Editions (HK) Ltd.

www.tuttlepublishing.com

Copyright © 2010 Graeme John Lund

Library of Congress Cataloging-in-Publication Data

Lund, Graeme John.
  The essential karate book : for white belts, black belts and all karateka in between / Graeme John Lund.
    p. cm.
  Includes index.
  ISBN 978-0-8048-4111-5 (pbk.)
  1. Karate. I. Title.
  GV1114.3.L86 2009
  796.815'3--dc22
                          2009036276

ISBN: 978-0-8048-4111-5

Distribued by:

North America, Latin America & Europe
Tuttle Publishing
364 Innovation Drive, North Clarendon, VT 05759-9436 U.S.A.
Tel: 1 (802) 773-8930 Fax: 1 (802) 773-6993
info@tuttlepublishing.com l www.tuttlepublishing.com

Japan
Tuttle Publishing
Yaekari Building, 3rd Floor, 5-4-12 Osaki, Shinagawa-ku, Tokyo 141 0032
Tel: (81) 3 5437-0171 Fax: (81) 3 5437-0755
sales@tuttle.co.jp l www.tuttle.co.jp

Asia Pacific
Berkeley Books Pte. Ltd., 61 Tai Seng Avenue #02-12, Singapore 534167
Tel: (65) 6280-1330 Fax: (65) 6280-6290
inquiries@periplus.com.sg l www.periplus.com

First edition   15 14 13 12 11   6 5 4 3 2   1112EP
Printed in Hong Kong

The Tuttle Story
"Books to Span the East and West"

Most people are surprised when they learn that the world's largest publisher of books on Asia had its beginnings in the tiny American state of Vermont. The company's founder, Charles Tuttle, came from a New England family steeped in publishing, and his first love was books—especially old and rare editions.

Tuttle's father was a noted antiquarian dealer in Rutland, Vermont. Young Charles honed his knowledge of the trade working in the family bookstore, and later in the rare books section of Columbia University Library. His passion for beautiful books—old and new—never wavered through his long career as a bookseller and publisher.

After graduating from Harvard, Tuttle enlisted in the military and in 1945 was sent to Tokyo to work on General Douglas MacArthur's staff. He was tasked with helping to revive the Japanese publishing industry, which had been utterly devastated by the war. After his tour of duty was completed, he left the military, married a talented and beautiful singer, Reiko Chiba, and in 1948 began several successful business ventures.

To his astonishment, Tuttle discovered that postwar Tokyo was actually a book-lover's paradise. He befriended dealers in the Kanda district and began supplying rare Japanese editions to American libraries. He also imported American books to sell to the thousands of GIs stationed in Japan. By 1949, Tuttle's business was thriving, and he opened Tokyo's very first English-language bookstore in the Takashimaya Department Store in Ginza, to great success. Two years later, he began publishing books to fulfill the growing interest of foreigners in all things Asian.

Though a Westerner Charles Tuttle was hugely instrumental in bringing a knowledge of Japan and Asia to a world hungry for information about the East. By the time of his death in 1993, he had published over 6,000 books on Asian culture, history and art—a legacy honored by Emperor Hirohito in 1983 with the "Order of the Sacred Treasure," the highest honor Japan bestows upon non-Japanese.

The Tuttle company today maintains an active backlist of some 1,500 titles, many of which have been continuously in print since the 1950s and 1960s—a great testament to Charles Tuttle's skill as a publisher. More than 60 years after its founding, Tuttle Publishing is more active today as at any time in its history, still inspired by Charles' core mission—to publish fine books to span the East and West and provide a greater understanding of each.

CONTENTS

DEDICATION

This book is dedicated to my father, John Clive Lund, who taught me, by example, without ever having heard of them, the five maxims of karate—character, sincerity, effort, etiquette and self-control.

ACKNOWLEDGMENTS

Thank you to my two senseis: Karl von der Marwitz and Steven Johnson, for making karate a pleasure and for encouraging dedication, knowledge and understanding of karate. Thank you to Kyoshi Claude Johnson for your inspirational warrior spirit. Thank you to Sensei Simon Kidd and to Kyoshi Pat Hayley for opening my eyes to the hidden power behind the ancient techniques. Thank you to my fellow karateka who have trained and fought with me and in so doing made me think faster and deeper. Thank you to Nicky Roote and Ansie Strydom for teaching me so much about the human body and for your contributions to making this book more thorough.

FOREWORD

I am deeply honored that Mr. Lund asked me to write this foreword for his latest work, *The Essential Karate Book*.

It has been my fortune (or should I say fate) to be involved in the fighting arts since 1976. During my precious free time, when not teaching or training, I spend a lot of time doing research and studying various combat systems. During this time I have come across many misrepresented aspects of fighting arts such as karate. My use of the term "misrepresented" is not intended to belittle the sincerity of those authors who have written extensively about the technical and historical aspects of Karate, but to draw the reader's attention to the fact that the origins of Okinawan Karate have become unnecessarily shrouded in so much myth.

To quote one of the great masters of karate, Gichin Funakoshi:

Karate-do is a noble martial art, and you can rest assure that those who take pride in breaking boards or smashing tiles, or who boast of being able to perform outlandish feats like stripping the flesh or plucking out ribs, really know nothing about karate. They are playing around in the leaves and branches of a great tree, without the slightest concept of the trunk.

Having studied and trained in karate for more than 20 years I can honestly say that, for too many people, karate is a mystery or worse: associated with screaming and chopping and wearing pajama-like clothes. Little do they realize that karate is an in-depth study of physical skills associated with intense mental discipline.

My first impression of Mr. Lund's book was that the book is a true reflection of that which every beginner student of karate should know and get exposed to—an introduction into the world of karate. *The Essential Karate Book* is also a must for all karate instructors as it breaks down some of the complex "mysteries" into simple illustrations *and* explanations. A well-known Japanese maxim says, *Kantan na mono yoku kachi o seisu*—"The balance between victory and defeat often hangs on simple matters."

The breadth of Mr. Lund's viewpoints and research makes his analysis and reflection the perfect framework for rethinking your personal study of karate. His writing, while in-depth, is not so extensive that it becomes boring. Rather, he finds interesting ways to stimulate students' minds in order to lead them to conclusions and clarity.

I know this book will be sought after and digested by all those who are interested in karate and its history, practice, and underlying concepts. Mr. Lund's book will appeal to many people, from instructors and students to the enthusiast whose aim is to learn and teach the full potential of the body and mind in the art of combat.

MORNÉ SWANEPOEL

Morné Swanepoel is a Black Belt Magazine *contributor and is one of the foremost mixed martial arts and reality-based combat trainers in the world.*

INTRODUCTION

Accidents happen. At the time, these horrible incidents appear to be disastrous and they often leave us in despair. However, our human nature soon kicks in and we look to the future and begin rebuilding. Many a success has risen from the wreckage of a personal catastrophe because we realize that we have a wealth of knowledge and experience on which to base our new found hope. This book originated in disaster, a personal injury that I suffered in early 2007 that prevented me from practicing karate. In my frustration I started making notes of what I had learned and found that I enjoyed writing about karate almost as much as I enjoyed practicing karate.

My initial intention was to simply record my knowledge for future reference but as I delved into seventeen years of experience I soon realized that my notes could be of use to others. One of the problems that Westerners face when doing karate is that their minds are not geared to learn from acts or from instruction. Western education has been the product of books, notes and research in libraries and on the Internet, all recorded neatly so that future reference is easy. It is very common for karateka to learn incorrect pronunciation, interpretation, translation, technique and sequence simply because they have no written point of reference. Instruction will vary from sensei to sensei and from dojo to dojo and, not having any written records, many instructions are simply forgotten. Adding fuel to the fire are the huge number of styles of karate each with their own teaching methods and terminology. Hopefully this book will help overcome these problems.

The number of karate styles is vast and continues to grow each year. However, they all have a common origin, the island of Okinawa, and their fundamental characteristics are much the same. Today, *Shorin-ryu* is the style that most resembles the karate practiced by the founding masters in the late eighteen hundreds and early nineteen hundreds.

The content of this book does not favor any one style or organization but does give specific information on *Goju-ryu, Shito-ryu, Shotokan, Wado-ryu* and *Shorin-ryu*. In addition, it is only the rules and regulations of the World Karate Federation (WKF) that are included in this book for the simple reason that the WKF is favored by the International Olympic Committee.

Of further importance is that many of the techniques shown is this book will vary from style to style. For example the position of the forearm on completion of an *age-uke* in *Shotokan* will be slightly different to that in *Shorin-ryu* and the *zenkutsu-dachi* of *Shotokan* are much deeper than those of *Shorin-ryu*. The techniques shown in this book are a guideline only and the *hanshis* of each style may use variations of these.

Should you wish to participate in competitive karate there are three main karate organizations. These are: World Karate Federation (WKF), World Karate Confederation (WKC) and World Union of Karate-do Organizations (WUKO).

WKF is recognized by the International Olympic Committee (IOC) as being responsible for karate competition in the Olympic games. Karate, however, does not yet have Olympic status. In the 117th IOC Session of July 2005, karate received more than half of the votes, but not the two-thirds majority needed to become an official Olympic sport. WKF accepts only one organization per country and only represents *Shotokan*, *Shito-ryu*, *Goju-Ryu* and *Wado-Ryu*. Other styles may join WKF but they may only perform the katas of these four styles.

WUKO offers the different styles and federations a world body that they may join without having to compromise their style or size. WUKO accepts more than one federation or association per country and the styles listed by WUKO include *Goju-ryu*, *Shito-ryu*, *Shotokan*, *Wado-ryu*, *Shorin-ryu*, *Uechi-ryu*, *Kyokushinkai* and *Budokan*.

WKC offers an option where all the different styles and federations can join a world body and fraternity, which does not require a change to their style. WKC accepts more than one federation or association per country. Any non-profit and non-political karate federation, association or other such group may be a member of WKC. They must have legal status, a democratic structure and comply with the aims and purpose of WKC. WKC does not judge or interfere with the internal structures or politics of its members.

Over the many years that I have been involved in martial arts I have trained in a number of different styles of karate including *Shotokan, Isshin-ryu* and *Shorin-ryu* as well having attended various courses in close quarter combat. In putting this book together I have taken information gathered from many different styles and teachers and put it into writing.

I hope that you find pleasure and assistance in reading this book.

SENSEI GRAEME LUND

Young karateka lined up and ready to receive their kumite medals.

A judge sitting in the corner of a dojo during a kumite bout.

A referee in a kumite bout.

Men's division competitors performing a unison kata.

Competitors, judges and referees presenting themselves at the start of a tournament.

Women's open kumite event.

CHAPTER 1

HISTORY

DEVELOPMENT OF KARATE

The exact origins of karate are lost in the mists of time and the smoke of war. We do know that karate originated in Okinawa but it is very difficult to tell the true story about the development of the Okinawan martial arts for two reasons. First, almost all written documents concerning Okinawan history and martial arts were destroyed during the American invasion of Okinawa in the Second World War. The second reason is that the martial arts were often practiced in secret and the techniques were passed on through word of mouth rather than in writing. Many martial artists conducted their training in secret as they did not want the state, the enemy or other martial artists to know what they were doing or what techniques they had developed.

As with most parts of the world, Okinawa was exposed to much war, invasion, internal strife and the odd despotic government and, just as in Europe, Africa, America, or Asia, new methods of fighting and war were developed. If the Romans were the masters of siege warfare and the British the masters of marine warfare then the Okinawans were the masters of unarmed combat and the development of weapons from seemingly harmless farming and fishing imple-

Okinawa is strategically positioned off the coast of China and close to Japan. This map shows the location of the three cities most influential in the development of karate.

ments. Just as the British became rulers of the oceans because of circumstances, so too did the Okinawans become masters of their art.

It is generally thought that there were four major factors in the development of karate. The first was an indigenous Okinawan martial art called *te* of which very little is known. The second was the influence of Chinese martial arts, which were combined with *te*. The third major influence was the development of the Okinawan warrior class in the thirteenth century and the fourth and final being the banning of weapons over much of Okinawa's history.

TE

In its earliest stages of development karate was a form of closed fist fighting which the Okinawans called *te*, or "hand." Thanks to the wars and weapons bans experienced in Okinawa this art continued to develop, mostly in secret in the cities of Shuri, Naha and Tomari. Interestingly, these towns are only a few kilometers apart but each was a center for a different element of society. Shuri, being the capital, was home to Okinawa's king and the nobles, Naha was the center of business and merchants and Tomari was the main town of the agriculture and fishing industries. Different forms of self-defense developed within each city and subsequently became known as *Shuri-te*, *Naha-te* and *Tomari-te*. Collectively they were called *Okinawa-te* or *tode*, "Chinese hand." Chinese influence was introduced and Chinese names were adopted. Karate eventually became divided into two main groups, namely: *Shorin-Ryu*, which developed around Shuri and Tomari, and *Shurei-ryu*, whose home was in Naha. The differences between these arts was one of emphasis and not kind. *Shorin-ryu* was quick and linear with natural breathing while *Shorei-ryu* emphasized steady, rooted movements and breathing synchronized with movements, similar to today's *Goju-ryu*.

CHINESE MARTIAL ARTS

Chinese martial arts can thank Bodhidharma for their origin. Bodhidharma was an Indian Buddhist monk who arrived in Shaolin-si (small forest temple), China, from India over 2,000 years ago. He taught Zen Buddhism and introduced a systematized set of exercises designed to strengthen the mind and body, exercises that allegedly marked the beginning of the *Shaolin* style of temple boxing. These teachings became the basis of Chinese martial arts. In Japan, Bodhidharma is known as Daruma. As with *te*, the Chinese arts developed over time, and when the Chinese started exerting influence over Okinawa these arts were quite different from the days of Bodhidharma.

A Chinese military envoy to Okinawa, records refer to him as Kusanku, had a major impact on the development of Karate when he introduced Chinese martial art techniques to the Okinawans. In fact the word *Shorin-ryu* means "small forest style" which has its origins in the days of Bodhidharma and his work at the "small forest temple."

The Chinese character used to write *tode* could also be pronounced "*kara*" thus the name *te* was replaced with *kara te-jutsu* or "Chinese hand art" by the Okinawan masters. This was later changed to *karate-do* by Gichin Funakoshi who adopted an alternate meaning for the Chinese character for *kara*, "empty." From this point on the term karate came to mean "empty hand." The *do* in *karate-do* means "way" or "path," and is indicative of the discipline and philosophy of karate with moral and spiritual connotations.

OKINAWAN NOBILITY

Most of Okinawan nobles, from the thirteenth century onwards, were required to work as officers in the army or police force where they kept law and order and received wages from the king for this service. No other occupation was allowed and thus they had no other source of income. At some point in time, this wage became insufficient to feed their families and many of them were reduced to beggary. In 1724, in order to solve this problem, the nobles were granted permission to become merchants, farmers, or craftsmen. Many of them left the state service and adopted a completely new lifestyle, including that of farming. After a century and a half, following the Meiji revolution, Okinawan nobles (as well as Japanese samurai) had their privileges revoked, including the right to carry swords, and those nobles that had remained on the state payroll were deprived of their wages. Members of the royal family worked as teamsters and night watchmen. Princes became hewers of wood and sellers of pigs in the marketplace. Many of the nobility moved into villages. The farmers, of course, weren't always happy with their new neighbors and they tried to drive them off the village's lands. These efforts often resulted in fighting. The number of thieves and robbers also increased in the countryside where food was scarce. As a result, "farmer-princes" had to refresh their fighting skills.

The nobility, of course, would have preferred to fight with their swords rather than with their bare hands, but they were prohibited from carrying weapons. But what does a warrior do when he can't use his weapons? He arms himself with anything in reach.

As many of the Okinawan weapons originate from farm implements it is often thought that peasants and farmers developed *kubudo*, the Okinawan art of weapons. This, however, is not entirely true. Certain weapons, in particular the *bo*, *kamma*, *ekku*, *nunchaku* and *tonfa*, were farm and fishing implements, but it was the nobles of Okinawa, and not the peasants, who developed the techniques that turned these implements into lethal weapons. The nobles formalized their techniques and added their expertise with these "weapons" to their unarmed fighting skills.

Banning of Weapons

Weapons were banned in Okinawa on numerous occasions. The first was in 1429 when King Sho Hashi founded the Sho dynasty by uniting the three principalities and establishing the Ryukyu kingdom with the city of Shuri as its capitol. Sho Hashi now had a string of islands with a number of united domains, but not a single country. Each lord still sat in his own castle, governed his fiefdom by himself, had his own army, imposed his own taxes, and had his own code of law and courts. The process of uniting these often warring domains into a single country took 50 years to complete. Sho Hashi's successor, King Sho Shin, turned the domains into a single country with one government, one army, and a single code of laws.

To reduce the possibility of a revolt in Okinawa, Sho Shin declared a prohibition against carrying weapons. Only the king's army and nobles were allowed to carry weapons and no one but the king could possess considerable amounts of weapons. As a result, the king's army became the only one on Okinawa.

Around 1580 new laws were passed that prohibited the possession or the carrying of weapons and in 1609, the Satsuma samurai clan attacked and swept the Okinawan defenses. The Japanese continued to enforce the laws that prevented the carrying of weapons.

The Shuri Castle was originally founded sometime during the thirteenth or fourteenth century.

NINETEENTH AND TWENTIETH CENTURY

Karate, as we know it today, has its origins in the nineteenth century and can be accredited to a few influential martial artists, all of whom were members of the elite royal palace guard. In 1806, "Tode" Sakugawa (1782–1838), who had studied pugilism and staff (*bo*) fighting in China, started teaching a fighting art in the city of Shuri that he called "*Karate-no-sakugawa*." Around the 1820's, Sakukawa's most significant student, Sokon Matsumura (1809–1899), who was also commander of the royal palace guard, taught a synthesis of *te* (*Shuri-te* and *Tomari-te*) and *Shaolin* styles that became known as *Shorin-ryu* ("Small Forest Style").

Matsumura taught his karate to Anko Itosu (1831–1915), among others. Itosu adapted two kata, or forms, as they are known in English, he had learned from Matsumara, namely *Kusanku* and *Chiang Nan*, to create the *Pinan* forms ("*Heian*" in Japanese, as the symbols can be read differently) as simplified kata for beginning students. In 1901 he was instrumental in getting karate introduced into Okinawa's public schools. These forms were taught to children at the elementary-school level. Itosu is also credited with taking the large *Naihanchi* form ("*Tekki*" in Japanese) and breaking it into the three well-known modern forms *Naihanchi Shodan*, *Naihanchi Nidan*, and *Naihanchi Sandan*.

Itosu's influence in karate is very broad. The forms he created for beginners are common across nearly all forms of karate. His students included some of the most well known karate practitioners, including Chosin Chibana, Gichin Funakoshi, Kenwa Mabuni, and Motobu Choki. He is sometimes known as the "grandfather of modern karate."

Modern karate consists of a huge variety of styles, most of which fall under the four recognized by the World Karate Federation (WKF). These four styles include *Shotokan*, *Wado-ryu*, *Shito-ryu* and *Goju-ryu*. The founders of both *Shotokan* and *Shito-ryu*, namely Gichin Funakoshi and Kenwa Mabuni respectively, were students of Anko Itosu. Hironori Ohtsuka, the founder of *Wado-ryu*, started his martial arts training with *jujitsu* and at a later age trained under Gichin Funukoshi, Kenwa Mabuni and Motobu Choki. *Goju-ryu's* founder was Higashionna Kanryo and his style of karate was a combination of *Naha-te* and a variation of *kung fu*.

The traditions and style of *Shorin-ryu* were continued by Chosen Chibana and are still practiced in Okinawa and the world.

KARATE ORIGINATORS AND GRAND MASTERS

Satunushi "Tode" Sakugawa (1762–1843)

Sakugawa is recognized as one of the most important figures in the history of karate as he was one of the first martial artists to blend the elements of *te* with *tode* (a form of Chinese boxing), hence his nickname, into what is today known as karate.

Born in Shuri, Sakugawa began his martial arts training as a youth under Peichin Takahara, a local astronomer and monk and later also trained with the know famous Kusanku. Thanks to the influence of Kusanku he made numerous visits to China were he trained in a variety of martial arts including *kempo* and *bojutsu*.

It was Sakugawa who developed the kata *Kusanku*, the bo kata *Sakugawa No Kun*, and the concept of the *dojo kun* (dojo etiquette).

Sokon "Bushi" Matsumura (1798–1890)

Matsumura is considered the father of all karate styles that originated in Okinawa. He was born into a prominent family in Shuri and is recorded as being a good scholar and athlete. As was customary for his status at the time, he learned the fundamentals of the *te* as a young boy. Later in life he began his formal martial arts training under Sakugawa where he learned many of his techniques and kata.

Matsumura served as a bodyguard and martial arts instructor to the last three Ryukyuan kings and was one of the last people to be given the title *Bushi*, meaning warrior, by a king. During this time he made a number of official visits to China and Japan where he studied Chinese boxing and Japanese swordsmanship.

Following retirement from service to the royal family, Matsumura taught karate in Shuri where he systematized *Shuri-te* into what became known as *Shorin-ryu*. Among many noteworthy students were Yasutsune Itosu, Kentsu Yabu, Chomo Hanashiro, Gichin Funakoshi, Chotoku Kyan, and Nabe Matsumura.

Matsumura is credited with the development of the katas *Chinto*, *Wansu*, *Passai* and *Seisan*.

Yasutsune Itosu (1830–1914)

Arguably one of the greatest karate teachers ever, Itosu simplified many of the ancient katas, created several new ones of his own and pioneered teaching methods that would revolutionize the art by making its study easier and less dangerous for future generations. For this, he is recognized as the father of modern karate.

Itosu is another of the old masters who was born in Shuri. He spent many years training under Matsumura as well as several other teachers including those from Tomari and Naha. Itosu was not only a great karateka but was also educated in Chinese and Japanese literature and served as a translator to Sho Tai, the last of the Ryukyuan kings, until Sho Tai's fall from power in 1879.

Perhaps the most significant of Itosu's contributions to modern karate was his influence in introducing karate into the physical education curriculum of the Okinawan public school system. By doing this he changed the perception of karate from being a secretive and feudalistic killing art into a healthy sporting art that could also be used for self-defense.

Itosu created the original *Pinan* (*Heian*) katas, *shodan* through *godan*, practiced today in various styles of karate. It was Itosu's students, including Gichin Funakoshi and Kenwa Mabuni, who went on to form some of the biggest styles of karate found today. Some of his other famous students include Chomo Hanashiro, Chosin Chibana, Kentsu Yabu, Choki Motobu and Shigeru Nakamura.

Kanryo Higashionna (1851–1915)

Higashionna was a contemporary and friend of Itosu and is also regarded as one of the most influential karate instructors in Okinawan history. As a leading developer and master of *Naha-te*, Higashionna laid the foundation for *Goju-ryu*, which was subsequently formalized by his senior student, Chojun Miyagi.

Higashionna (or Higaonna) was born in Naha to a very poor family. He learned the basics of *te* as a youth and began studying *tode* at the age of sixteen under a local teacher named Arakaki. At the age of twenty-two, he went to Fuchou, China where he remained for between ten to sixteen years mastering Chinese boxing. Upon his return to Okinawa, he began teaching his art while continuing to develop it into what became known as *Naha-te*. Higashionna is credited with introducing and popularizing the kata *Sanchin* on Okinawa, as well as the *Sanchin* method of breathing.

Among Higashionna's most important students were Chojun Miyagi, founder of *Goju-ryu*, and Kenwa Mabuni, founder of *Shito-ryu*.

Gichen Funakoshi (1868–1957)

Called "the grandfather of Japanese karate," Gichin Funakoshi founded *Shotokan*, one of the most popular styles of karate in the world today.

Born in Shuri, Funakoshi began his karate training under Yasutsune Asato and later Yasutsune Itosu, both students of the great Sokon "Bushi" Matsumura. Funakoshi also trained with Matsumura on occasion.

Unlike most karate masters of the time, Funakoshi was well-educated and brought a refined, philosophical approach to karate that attracted the attention of intellectuals and educators on the Japanese mainland. In 1922, he gave a demonstration at the *Butokuden* (Martial Virtues Hall) in Kyoto after which he remained in Japan to spread his art. At the age of fifty-three he embarked upon, what he came to consider, his destiny.

In his teaching, Funakoshi emphasized basic technique, kata training and perfection of the individual through *"do"* or "the way." He is credited with the famous saying *"Karate ni sente nashi*—There is no first attack in karate."

Kenwa Mabuni (1890–1952)

Mabuni was born into the *shizoku* (samurai) class and at the age of thirteen started his karate training under *Shuri-te* master Itosu and *Naha-te* master Higashionna. Mabuni combined elements of these two styles to form *Hanko-ryu* (half-hard style) which he later renamed in tribute to his teachers, using the Chinese character *shi* ("ito" in Itosu) and *to* ("higa" in Higashionna), to form *Shito-ryu*.

Mabuni trained karate in all parts of Okinawa until 1929 when he made a permanent move to Japan. Here he taught at the universities and police departments.

Chojun Miyagi (1888–1952)

Miyagi came after the generation of martial artists who grew up in the feudal system and had no connection to royalty. In fact he was the son of a wealthy shop owner in Naha. Miyagi began his training at age eleven under Ryuko Aragake through whom he later met Higashionna. He began training with Higashionna at age fourteen and stayed with him for fifteen years until the master's death in 1916. Shortly before Higashionna died, Miyagi went to China to study *kempo* for a year.

After Higashionna's death, Miyagi began to take on students and develop Higashionna's karate into his own style while blending in new elements he'd learned in China. He taught at the Prefecture Police School dojo, at the Naha Courthouse, the Prefecture Physical Culture Association, the Prefecture Teachers' Training College, and at numerous colleges and universities on the Japanese mainland. In addition, he taught in Hawaii and in Shanghai.

During a demonstration at the *Botukuden* on the Japanese mainland in 1937, Miyagi named his style *"go-ju,"* meaning hard-soft.

Hironori Ohtsuka (1892–1982)

Ohtsuka, whose father was a medical doctor, was born in Shimodate City, Japan. Ohtsuka was first introduced to martial arts by his great uncle, Chojiro Ebashi, a samurai warrior, who began teaching him *jujitsu*. When he was thirteen, he studied the style under Shinzaburo Nakayama, a grandmaster of *jujitsu*. He continued with his studies through school and university. In 1922 Ohtsuka met Gichin Funakoshi and began to learn more about karate while still continuing with his studies of *jujitsu*. Ohtsuka also studied other Japanese martial arts including judo, kendo and aikido. He blended the practical and useful elements of Okinawan karate with the techniques found in *jujitsu* and *kendo*, which led to the birth of kumite in karate. At this stage Ohtsuka thought that there was a need for this more dynamic and fluid type of karate to be taught, so he decided to leave Funakoshi to concentrate on developing his own style of karate—*Wado*. In 1934, *Wado-ryu* karate was officially recognized as an independent style of karate. Ohtsuka left his medical practice and became a full-time martial artist. In 1944, Ohtsuka was appointed Japan's Chief Karate Instructor.

Choki Motobu (1870–1944)

Choki Motobu is perhaps the most controversial of all great karate masters. He first gained notoriety as a bully and a braggart, and, later in life, despite adopting a more humble attitude, he was never able to outlive his earlier reputation.

Like his brother Choyu, Choki Motobu was born in Shuri, but, being his father's third son, was never taught the family's martial arts system. Instead he picked up the basics of *te* by peeking through the dojo fences and trained himself on the *makiwara*. He lifted rocks to develop his strength and earned the nickname "Saru" (monkey) for his exceptional leaping ability. He also practiced fighting by brawling in the streets every night with anyone who'd accommodate him. Though he briefly trained with Itosu and Matsumora, his over-aggressiveness caused both associations to be short-lived.

Late in life, Choki underwent a profound change in attitude. Seeking the true meaning of karate-do, he dedicated himself to a serious study of kata under Yabu Kentsu, one of the few men who'd ever beaten him in fighting.

Choki's favorite kata was *Naihanchi*, which he claimed was the only kata required for the mastery of karate. He remains best known for his *kumite*, and up until his death, other masters sent their students to him to learn his free-fighting techniques.

Choki Motobu's famous students include Shoshin Nagamine, founder of *Matsubayashi-ryu*, Shigeru Nakamura, founder of Okinawan *kempo*; and Tatsuo Shimabuku, founder of *Isshin-ryu*.

Chosin Chibana (1885–1969)

Chibana spent his life preserving Okinawan karate. He was born in Shuri and left school at the age of fifteen to study karate full time with Itosu where he remained for thirteen years until Itosu's death in 1914. Itosu was the only teacher Chibana ever had.

Chibana opened his first dojo at the age of thirty-four and taught karate exactly as Itosu had taught it to him. In 1933, he officially named the style *Kobashi Shorin-ryu* to differentiate it from the *Shorin-ryu* styles that had come down from Chotoku Kyan.

Chibana moved often, opening dojos and founding Karate clubs throughout Okinawa. From 1954 to 1958, he was chief karate instructor at the Shuri police station and, in 1956, was a founding member and first president of the Okinawan Karate-do Federation. Two years later, he helped found the Okinawan *Shorin-ryu* Karate-do Association and served as it's first president. In 1968, he received the *Kunyonto* Order of the Sacred Treasure from Emperor Hirohito.

Chibana always believed that karate should be taught as an art and not as a sport or as a mere form of exercise. He continually strived to better himself and, until his death at age eighty-four, believed he had much to learn.

CHAPTER 2

DOJO ETIQUETTE

Karate is a contact sport and students will eventually learn to kill an opponent with their bare hands. As such, karate is a potentially dangerous sport and to prevent unnecessary injuries karate dojos make use of very strict etiquette. This etiquette ensures that students respect each other, their sensei and themselves and that the lethal techniques that students learn are practiced in a very controlled environment. It is thanks to etiquette that karateka suffer relatively few serious injuries in a sport that aims to injure.

CLASS ETIQUETTE

Karate training begins and ends with rituals of etiquette. The following should always be practiced:

Shomen

The shomen is the front of the dojo and, traditionally, held a small *Shinto* shrine, the *dojo kun* and the *hata*. In most Western dojos the front of the dojo holds only symbolic importance and, in the tradition of karate, it is still shown respect.

Dojo Kun

The *dojo kun* are the basic rules of karate and were written by Satsunuku "Tode" Sakugawa. They are also known as *The Five Maxims of Karate*. Traditionally, the *dojo kun* is posted outside the dojo and at the *shomen*. Various styles of karate have modified these maxims, and, in some cases, added to them. Sakugawa's *dojo kun* are:

Character—Show inner strength through a strong Character.

Sincerity—Practice karate with Sincerity.

Effort—Train mind and body with every Effort possible.

Etiquette—Respect yourself and others and live the true spirit and Etiquette of Karate-Do.

Self-Control—Never abuse karate skills and strive for Self-Control. Violence should be the last resort.

Before Entering the Dojo

- Shoes must be removed and left outside the dojo.
- Karateka must be neatly and appropriately dressed before entering the dojo.
- All jewelery and watches must be removed before commencement of training. Place them in a secure location or leave them at home.
- Switch off all cellular telephones, pagers, alarms, and the like before entering the dojo.
- High levels of personal hygiene are to be maintained. Always wear clean clothing, keep nails short, cover any injuries, etc.

On the Dojo Floor

- *Rei*, which means bow, when entering or leaving the dojo. All bows are done with feet together, in a *heiko-dachi*, and facing the *shomen*.

Front and side view of the beginning position for the **rei**. **Rei** *begins in a* **heiko-dachi**.

Rei *from the front.*   **Rei** *from the side.*

- *Rei* when greeting another karateka.
- *Rei* at the start and finish of a paired training session.
- Students may not talk in class.
- Students may not cross the dojo between the sensei and the class. They are to cross the dojo behind the students.
- If the class is already in session when a student arrives, they are to warm up outside the dojo and when ready wait at the back of the dojo until called forward by the sensei.

Starting the Class

- Prior to the start of the class assume the *yoi* stance with senior karateka in the front row and the most senior karateka of each row on the right.

The **yoi** *stance.*

■ The sensei may request a formal bow. He will give the command *"seiza"* which means kneel.

This sequence of images shows the progression of movements in the formal bow.

- If the students are kneeling, the sensei may instruct them to meditate by saying "*mokusoh*" and when the meditation period is over he will say "*mokusoh yame.*"

- Whether kneeling or standing the sensei will then say "*shomen ni rei*" which means bow to the *shomen*, followed by "*sensei ni rei*" which means bow to the *sensei* and possibly "*otagai ni rei*" which means bow to the others. After each bow the students will say "*osu*" which is a form of greeting.

- If the class has been kneeling the sensei will instruct the class to rise. Strictly speaking, the person in the front right of the class rises first and then the next person in descending order of rank.

- The sensei will begin the warm up by saying "*judon tai so.*" Once the warm up is complete he will finish the warm up by saying "*judon u warimashta*" and bow to the class who will reply "*domo arigato.*"

Ending the Class

- The sensei may request a formal bow and give the command "*seiza.*"
- If the students are kneeling, the sensei may instruct them to meditate.
- The sensei may then request the class to recite the *dojo kun*.
- Whether kneeling or standing the sensei will then request the three bows.
- If the class has been kneeling the sensei will instruct the class to rise.
- The most senior karateka walks off the dojo followed, in descending order of rank, by the other students.

CLOTHING

Gi

Most martial artists use a *gi* in one form or another and the *gi* comes in two parts; the top and the pants. A karate and judo *gi* is completely white, a *kubudo gi* is brown and an aikido *gi* has black pants and a white top. A *gi* is generally made from cotton, has a very loose fit and has strong stitching. Okinawa has extremely hot and humid summers and the fabric and fit of a *gi* is ideally suited to this climate. It also works very well in the hot and humid environment of an enclosed dojo. The strength of a *gi* comes in handy when martial artists grapple with each other.

The *gi* pants are held around the waste by a draw cord while the *gi* top is held closed by knotting two pieces of material found on the inside of the *gi*. The belt further assists in keeping the *gi* top closed.

Club and/or style badges are generally sewn onto the *gi* and are positioned over the top left of the torso. If competing in international or national competitions, the national flag or regional colors may be worn on the top of the left sleeve.

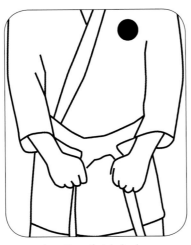

Location of style badge.

Location of the national flag.

Obi

An *obi*, the belt worn around the waist, not only signifies a karateka's level of training but helps to keep the *gi* top closed and also offers some protection to the body's vital organs from a strike on the lower back.

An *obi* is generally about 2.5m long. Ideally the *obi* should be able to fit three times around the waist of a karateka. See the diagrams on how to tie an *obi* on page 26.

When competing, participants in WKC events are required to have two belts, one blue and the other red, depending on the starting position. These coloured belts are worn regardless of the karateka's grading.

Mouthguard

Mouthguards are worn to protect the teeth, tongue and inside of the mouth from injury. They come in a variety of forms and can be molded to suite an individual's teeth. It is compulsory to wear a mouthguard when competing in *kumite* events.

Groin and Bust Protectors

As with mouth guards, it is compulsory for groin and bust protectors to be worn by male and female *kumite* competitors respectively when competing in *kumite* events.

Head, Arm, Shin and Instep Protectors

This protective gear is not compulsory and in many cases is forbidden in competitions. Certain dojos also discourage the use of these items in class as they do not allow the forearms, shins and instep to become conditioned to contact. They are usually worn by an individual who is in the final stages of preparation for a competition and who does not want to be injured or by a person who has extensive bruising on these areas and does not want to be further injured.

A groin protector.

A head protector.

Shin protectors inhibit contact.

Proper use of shin protectors.

Sparring Gloves

Sparring gloves are also compulsory when competing in kumite events and vary in color depending on the stipulations of the governing body. In WKF events competitors are required to have two pairs of gloves, one red and the other blue and in WKC competitors may only use white gloves.

Sparring gloves protect the wearer and the opponent.

HOW TO ADDRESS A KARATEKA

RANK	TITLE
First through tenth *kyu*	*Kohai*
First through fourth *dan*	*Sensei*
Fifth and sixth *dan*	*Renshi*
Seventh and eighth *dan*	*Kyoshi*
Ninth and tenth *dan*	*Hanshi*

Shihan is a term used to address a head of a style in a particular region.

SEQUENCE OF *OBI*

Different styles of karate award different color belts to signify different levels of training. Generally all styles begin with a white belt and issue a black belt when a karateka reaches a level of expertise and commitment that qualifies them to teach.

Shotokan

BELT	*KYU* (GRADE)	ESTIMATED TRAINING
White		
Orange	Ninth	Six months
Red	Eighth	Six months
Yellow	Seventh	Six months
Green	Sixth	Six months
Purple	Fifth	Six months
Purple/white	Fourth	Six months
second Purple	Third	One year
First brown	Second	One year
Second brown	First	One year
Third brown/white	First	One year
Black	First	One year

Shito-Ryu

BELT	*KYU* (GRADE)	ESTIMATED TRAINING
White		
Red		Two months
Red (one stripe)		Two months
Red (two stripes)		Two months
Yellow	Tenth	Two months
Orange	Ninth	Two months
Blue	Eighth	Two months
Purple	Seventh	Two months
Green	Sixth	Two months
Green (one stripe)	Fifth	Two months
Green (two stripes)	Fourth	Two months
Brown	Third	Three months
Brown (one stripe)	Second	Three months
Brown (two stripes)	First	Three months
Black with white stripe	*Sho Dan Ho*	One year

Gojo-Ryu

BELT	*KYU* (GRADE)	ESTIMATED TRAINING
White	Tenth	
Yellow	Ninth	Six months
Orange	Eighth	Six months
Orange	Seventh	Six months
Blue	Sixth	Six months
Blue	Fifth	Six months
Blue	Fourth	Six months
Green	Third	One year
Brown	Second	One year
Black	first	One year

Wado-Ryu

BELT	*KYU* (GRADE)	ESTIMATED TRAINING
White		
Red	Ninth	Six months
Yellow	Eighth	Six months
Orange	Seventh	Six months
Blue	Sixth	Six months
Green	Fifth	Six months
Purple	Fourth	Six months
First brown	Third	One year
Second brown	Second	One year
Third brown	First	One year
Black	First Dan	One year

Shorin-Ryu

BELT	*KYU* (GRADE)	ESTIMATED TRAINING
White		
Red Stripe		Six months
Yellow	Eighth	Six months
Orange	Seventh	Six months
Green	Sixth	Six months
Blue	Fifth	Six months
First Purple	Fourth	Six months
Second Purple	Third	One year
First Brown	Second	One year
Second Brown	First	One year
Black	First Dan	One year

HOW TO TIE AN *OBI*

There are many ways to tie an *obi* and they vary from one style of karate to another. The method used in Okinawa is shown here.

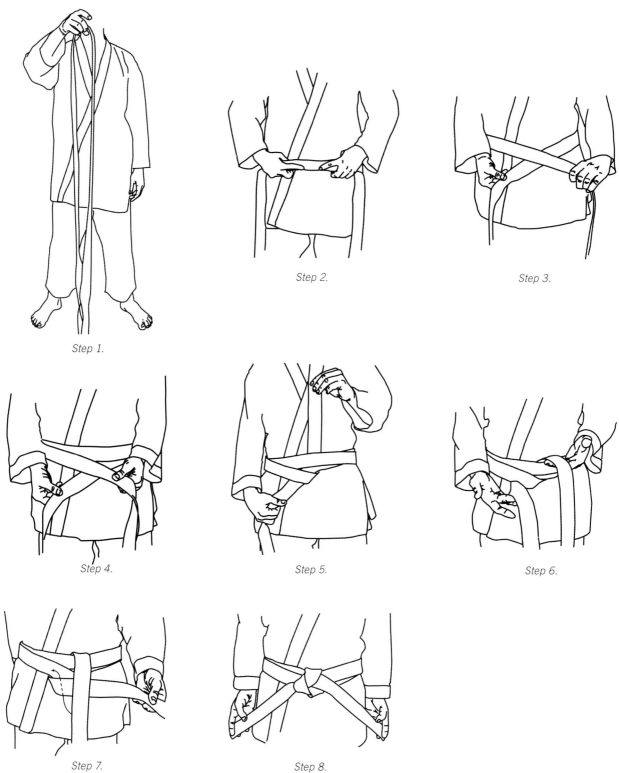

Step 1.

Step 2.

Step 3.

Step 4.

Step 5.

Step 6.

Step 7.

Step 8.

HOW TO FOLD A *GI*

A gi, particularly a heavy weight *gi*, is large and cumbersome and difficult to transport without creasing. These diagrams show how to effectively fold a *gi* into a compact bundle that doesn't result in creases.

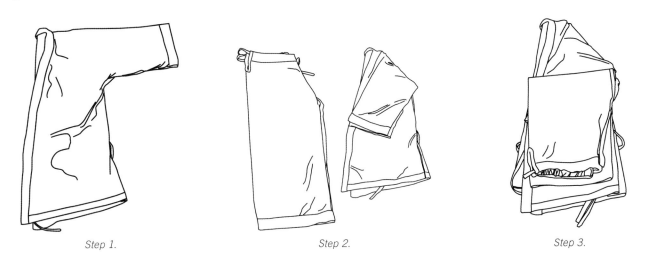

Step 1.   Step 2.   Step 3.

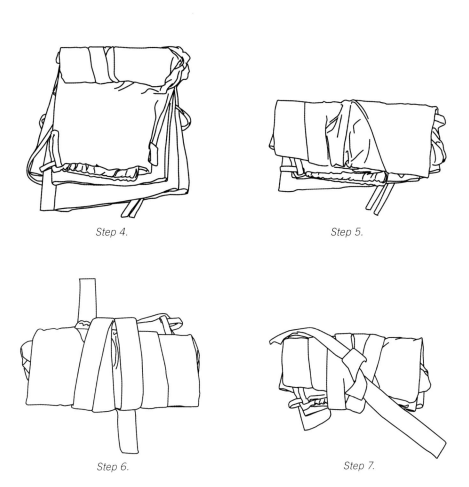

Step 4.   Step 5.

Step 6.   Step 7.

*A **kiai** serves several purposes.*

CHAPTER 3

FUNDAMENTALS OF KARATE

There are certain elements of karate that are fundamental to the sport and they have caused controversy in the past, particularly among Western religious groups who perceive these fundamental elements to be spiritual and contrary to Christianity. However, all of these elements have been explained through modern science and it has been found that they are practiced in Western sports too.

HARA OR *TAN DEN*

The *hara* is the physical center of gravity located in the abdomen three finger-widths below and two finger widths behind the navel and consists of a number of muscles namely the *Transversus Abdominus*, the *Multifidi*, the *Pelvic Floor* and the *Diaphragm*. In the Western culture these muscles are called the *Core* or the *Stabilizing Muscles*. All effective movement depends on the *hara* as without it we would simply be unbalanced and fall over. By optimizing the *hara* a karateka has a very stable platform from which to deliver a strike or ward off an attack. In addition, without using the *hara* correctly a karateka will not be able to perform a kata sequence or a *kumite* combination effectively.

KI

Ki is believed to be the latent energy stored in the *hara*. By optimizing the use of one's *hara* you are able to maximize the effect of the *ki*. Most martial art systems believe that the *ki* may be harnessed and used in combat. In fact every sport that requires balance makes use of this force.

KIME

This is the focus of the *ki* at the moment of impact of a block, strike or other form of contact. Effective *kime* comes with correct breathing and very simply a karateka will breath out while applying the technique and end the breath sharply at the same instant as the impact. This is not unique to martial arts as any tennis spectator will know. *Kime* is also used when the body receives a blow and by breathing out sharply at the moment the blow is landed, the body minimises the effect of the blow.

Proper breathing maximizes your impact.

Breathing correctly is very important in karate for a number of reasons other than creating *kime*. It improves endurance, allows the karateka to think faster and more effectively and, after vigorous exercise, allows the body to return to a normal level of heartbeat and breathing more rapidly. A karateka must focus on breathing as much as on the technique being performed. In time the *hara's* muscle memory will work automatically with the rest of the body and *kime* will happen without conscious thought.

KIAI

Kiai is the term that commonly refers to a short yell that some martial artists shout before or during a fight or technique and it is this yell that releases the *kime*. Practical uses of *kiai* include: startling and demoralizing an opponent, priming the mind for combat by "amping up," protecting the upper body from a strike by providing an escape route for exhalation of air, protecting the lower body by rapidly contracting the transverse abdominals and other core muscles thus shielding the internal organs and also to provide a solid support for striking techniques.

KOSHI

Koshi refers to the effective use of the hips in karate. The hip joint of the front leg is the pivotal point or axis and moving the other hip around this axis with focused speed and energy in conjunction with blocks, strikes or take downs adds vastly more power to these defensive or attacking movements.

By combining *koshi* with *kiai*, a karateka may appear to have supernatural strength and power. In reality this is simply extraordinarily good biomechanics.

MUSHIN

Mushin means "mind of no mind" and refers to a state that highly experienced martial artists achieve when in combat—it is the state in which every action and reaction occurs without any conscious thought. The fighter feels no anger, fear, or ego, they simply do what feels best. A karateka needs to train for many years, practicing combinations of movements and techniques many hundreds of times until they can be performed without conscious thought.

FUNDAMENTALS OF *SHOTOKAN*

The emblem for **Shotokan**.

Shotokan techniques are characterized by deep, long stances that provide stability, powerful movements and also help strengthen the legs. *Shotokan* is a hard style with strong, powerful moves being more prevalent than slower, more flowing motions. The stances of *Shotokan* are also more upright than those of other styles, especially those with close links to original Okinawan style. *Shotokan* is linear in its movements.

Shoto is the pen name used by Gichin Funakoshi, the founder of *Shotokan* and means "pine wave," *kan* means "house," *Shotokan* is therefor the name given to a hall where Funakoshi trained his students.

Before his students established the Japan Karate Association, Funakoshi laid out the *Twenty Precepts of Karate*, which form the foundations of *Shotokan*. Within these twenty principles, based heavily on *Bushido* and *Zen*, lies the philosophy of *Shotokan*.

1. Never forget: karate begins and ends with respect
2. There is no first attack in karate
3. Karate supports righteousness
4. First understand yourself, then understand others
5. The art of developing the mind is more important than the art of applying technique
6. The mind needs to be freed
7. Trouble is born of negligence / ignorance
8. Do not think karate belongs only in the dojo
9. Karate training requires a lifetime
10. Transform everything into karate; therein lays its exquisiteness
11. Karate is like hot water, if you do not give it heat constantly, it will again become cold water
12. Do not think that you have to win, rather think you do not have to lose
13. Transform yourself according to the opponent
14. The outcome of the fight depends on one's control
15. Imagine one's arms and legs as swords
16. Once you leave the shelter of home, there are a million enemies
17. Postures are for the beginner; later they are natural positions
18. Perform the kata correctly; the real fight is a different matter
19. Do not forget control of the dynamics of power, the elasticity of the body and the speed of the technique
20. Apply the way of karate to all things. Therein lies its beauty.

Individual styles of *Shotokan* include:

- JKA
- JSKA
- *Shotokai*
- ITKF—International Traditional Karate Federation
- SRKHIA (WSKA)—*Shotokan-kase-ha* Instructor Academy
- SKIF—*Shotokan* Karate-do International Federation
- JKS—Japan Karate *Shotorenmei*
- KWF—*Karatenomichi* World Federation

FUNDAMENTALS OF *SHITO-RYU*

The emblem for **Shito-Ryu**.

Shito-ryu is a combination of all the original karate styles of *Shuri*, *Naha* and *Tomari-te*. It includes deep stances, powerful attacks but also circular hand movements and eight directional body movements. *Shito-ryu* is a fast style that is also artistic and powerful.

Kenwa Mabuni, the founder of *Shito-ryu* also developed the five rules of defense known as *Uke no go gensoku*, *Uke no go genri* or *Uke no go ho*:

- *rakka*, "falling petals"—The art of blocking with such force and precision as to completely destroy the opponent's attacking motion.
- *ryusui*, "running water"—The art of flowing around the attacker's motion, and through it, soft blocking.
- *ku-ushin*, "elasticity"—This is the art of bouncing back, storing energy while recoiling from the opponent's attack, changing or lowering stance only to immediately unwind and counterattack.
- *teni*, "transposition"—*Teni* is the use of all eight directions of movement, most importantly stepping away from the line of attack.
- *hangeki,* "counterattack"—A *hangeki* defense is an attack that at the same time deflects the opponent's attack before it can reach the defender.

Individual styles of *Shito-Ryu* include:

- *Shito-kai*
- *Seito Shito-ryu*
- *Shuko-kai*
- *Itosu-kai*
- *Seishin-kai*
- *Kuniba-kai*

- *Hagashi-ha*
- *Inoue-ha Shito-ryu Keinshin-kai*
- *Shiroma Shito-ryu*
- *Kotaka-ha Shito-ryu*
- *Sanku-kai*
- *Genbu-kai*

- *Hokushin*
- *San-shin-kan*
- *Kurokana-ha Shito-ryu Kai*
- *Sieto-kai*

FUNDAMENTALS OF *GOJU-RYU*

The emblem for **Goju-Ryu**.

Goju-ryu means "hard-soft style" in Japanese and as such uses a combination of hard and soft techniques. The harder elements of *Goju-ryu* are the attacks such as kicks and strikes while the softer circular techniques are those of blocking and controlling the opponent, including locks, grappling, takedowns and throws. The movements in *Goju-ryu* are linear and circular. More than most styles of karate, *Goju-ryu* emphasizes breathing and the strength and power that it gives to karate. *Goju-ryu* also advances methods that include body strengthening and conditioning, distancing, stickiness, power generation, and partner drills.

Individual styles of *Goju-Ryu* include:

- IOGKF
- *Goju-kai*
- *Jundokan*

- *Kenshikai*
- *Meibukan*
- *Seito Goju-ryu*

- *Sengukan*
- *Shobukan*
- *Shoreikan*

- *Jinbukan*
- *Shodokan*
- *Isshin-ryu*

FUNDAMENTALS OF *WADO-RYU*

The techniques of *Wado-ryu* appear very similar to other styles of karate but most of the underlying principles have been derived from *Shindo Yoshin Ryu*, a style of *jujutsu*. An example is where other styles of karate may use a powerful block to defeat an opponent's strike, *Wado-ryu* emphasizes moving the entire body out of the line of attack while taking up a position that will gain the practitioner an advantage over his opponent, this is the principle of *taisabaki*. *Wado-ryu* adherents believe in moving with, rather than against, the attacker. *Wa* can be read to mean harmony. *Do* is a Japanese term for way, *ryu* simply means style. *Wa,* or harmony, shouldn't be interpreted as pacifism in any way. It is merely the acknowledgment that yielding is sometimes more effective than brute strength.

Individual styles of *Wado-Ryu* include:
- *Wadokai*
- *Wado Kokusai*
- *Wadoryu Remei*

FUNDAMENTALS OF *SHORIN-RYU*

The emblem for **Shorin-Ryu.**

Shorin-ryu is generally characterized by natural breathing, relatively narrow and high stances and direct, rather than circular movements. *Shorin-Ryu Kyudokan* is the one exception as circular movements are one of its fundamentals. *Shorin-ryu* is a traditional Okinawan style with the *hanbo dojo's* being in Okinawa.

Individual styles of *Shorin-Ryu* include:
- *Shobayashi*
- *Ryukyu Hon Kenpo*
- *Matsumura* Orthdox *Shorin-ryu*
- *Seidokan*
- *Kobayashi Shorin-ryu (Shido-kan and Shorinkan)*
- *Kyudokan*
- *Matsubayashi-ryu*
- *Okinawa kenpo*
- *Sukunaihayashi (Shorin-ryu Seibukan)*
- *Shorin-ryu Shorinkan*

KARATE *KANJI*

Kanji are the Chinese characters that are used, among others, in the modern Japanese logographic writing system. The Japanese term *kanji* literally means "*Han* characters." *Kanji* are read from top to bottom but when used in Western books they are read from left to right.

The word "karate" was used verbally for some time before it was written. The first use of the word karate in print is attributed to Anko Itosu, who wrote it with the *kanji* (Tang Dynasty hand). The Tang Dynasty of China ended over 1,000 years ago, but the *kanji* representing karate remained in use in Okinawa as a way to referring to China generally, thus karate generally meant "Chinese hand" or "martial art from China."

The use of "Chinese hand," reflects the Chinese influence on karate. In 1905, Hanashiro Chomo (1869–1945) began using a homophone of the logogram pronounced "kara" by replacing the character meaning "Tang Dynasty" with the character meaning "empty." In 1933, the Okinawan art of karate was recognized as a Japanese martial art by the Japanese Martial Arts Committee known as the *Butoku Kai* and, two years later, in 1935, the masters of the various styles of karate conferred to decide a new name for their art. They decided to call their art "karate" written in Japanese characters as 空手 (empty hand). This *kanji* remains in use today.

*Demonstration of the **kosa-dachi** stance.*

CHAPTER 4

STANCES, MOVEMENT, AND BLOCKS

STANCES

Karate techniques are performed effectively only when the applicable stance is adopted correctly. Correct posture adds stability, strength and power to stances. Strong stances with feet planted firmly, toes gripping the floor and good posture add stability, strength and power to movement, strikes, blocks and kicks.

Different stances are adopted for different means of attack and defense. Fighting stance (*kamae*) allows for rapid movement in all directions whether it is for blocking, punching, kicking, avoiding an attack or throwing your opponent to the floor. The cat stance (*neko-ashi-dachi*) is useful for kicking off the front leg or using the leg to block strikes or kicks. Lower stance (*zenkutsu-dachi*) is adopted when following through with a strike. Horse stance (*kiba-dachi*) gives great strength when resisting an opponent's forward movement, and also allows for strong side thrust kicks.

The stances shown in this chapter vary quite considerably from style to style. An example being that in *Shotokan*, the fists of a karateka must be the width apart of the individual's waist when standing at *yoi* in *hachiji-dachi*. In *Shorin-ryu* the fists are one fist width apart. Keep in mind that feet distance and posture will be slightly different for different physiques and that what works for a tall, thin karateka may not be optimum for a short, stocky karateka.

Types of Stances

The stances shown below are mostly those of the original Okinawan masters.

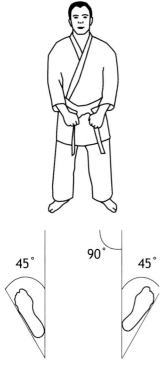

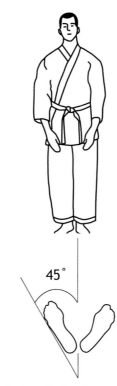

*Foot positioning diagram for the **hachiji-dachi** stance.*

*Foot positioning diagram for the **musubi-dachi** stance.*

*Foot positioning diagram for the **heiku-dachi** stance.*

*Demonstration of the **hachiji-dachi** stance.*

*Demonstration of the **musubi-dachi** stance.*

*Demonstration of the **heiku-dachi** stance.*

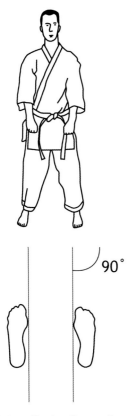

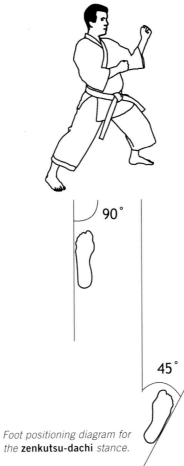

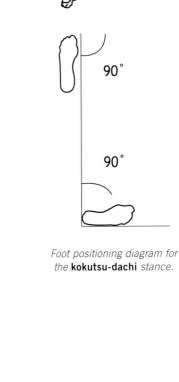

*Foot positioning diagram for the **heisuko-dachi** stance.*

*Foot positioning diagram for the **zenkutsu-dachi** stance.*

*Foot positioning diagram for the **kokutsu-dachi** stance.*

*Demonstration of the **heisuko-dachi** stance.*

*Demonstration of the **zenkutsu-dachi** stance.e.*

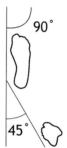

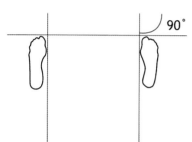

*Foot positioning diagram for the **kiba-dachi** stance.*

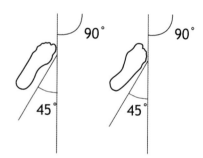

*Foot positioning diagram for the **kosa-dachi** stance.*

*Foot positioning diagram for the **nenama zenkutsu-dachi** stance.*

*Demonstration of the **kiba-dachi** stance.*

*Demonstration of the **kosa-dachi** stance.*

*Demonstration of the **nenama zenkutsu-dachi** stance.*

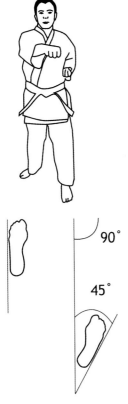

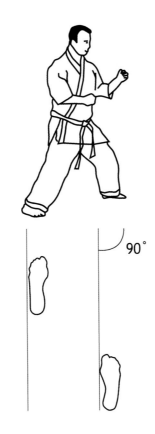

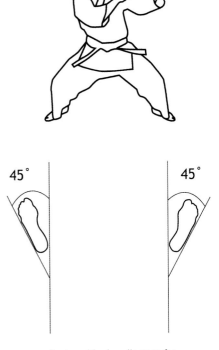

Foot positioning diagram for the **shizentai-dachi** *stance.*

Foot positioning diagram for the **ju-dachi/kamae** *stance.*

Foot positioning diagram for the **shiko-dachi** *stance.*

Demonstration of the **shizentai-dachi** *stance.*

Demonstration of the **ju-dachi/kamae** *stance.*

Demonstration of the **shiko-dachi** *stance.*

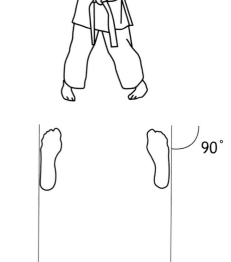

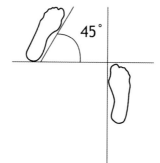

*Foot positioning diagram for the **neko-ashi-dachi** stance.*

*Foot positioning diagram for the **sanchin-dachi** stance.*

*Foot positioning diagram for the **naihanchi-dachi** stance.*

*Demonstration of the **neko-ashi-dachi** stance.*

*Demonstration of the **sanchin-dachi** stance.*

*Demonstration of the **naihanchi-dachi** stance.*

MOVEMENT

Basics of All Movement

All movements, whether changing stance, moving forward, backward or sideways or launching an attack must follow the same basic principles:

- All movement must be based on the fundamentals of karate, namely the *hara*, *ki*, *kime*, and, when necessary, end with a *kiai*. In other words, all movements begin in the *hara*, drawing on the *ki*, and end with *kime*. These fundamentals are put into place by contracting and releasing the muscles of the core.

- All movement must begin with hip movement, another of karate's fundamentals. This use of the hips, or *koshi*, ensures that every step, strike, kick or block is backed by the full weight of the body and not just the strength of the single limb. *Koshi* magnifies the impact of this movement more than ten fold and it is *koshi* that allows karateka to break boards, bricks, ice and bones.

- Breath with the movements, breathing in before and while performing the movement and breathing out sharply as the movement comes to an end. This outward breathing can be emphasised with a *kiai*.

- Move within the body's optimum dimensions. In other words, don't overcommit your body to a movement by extending too far with arms and legs and thus losing balance or exposing yourself to a counterattack.

- Ensure that you have both feet on the ground before moving your arms.

- Use both legs to move. Pull with the leg in the same direction the movement is going and push off with the leg that is following.

- Do not move the head unless absolutely necessary. Perhaps the only occasion when the head should be moved is to avoid a strike to the head when a full body movement cannot be used. The head, like the *hara*, is key to stability. By moving the head off center, the body loses much of its *kime*.

This is an enormous amount to remember and put into practice every time the body moves and it is precisely for this reason that karate takes years to learn. The old masters of karate developed repetitive training to ensure that when students were practicing a particular step, strike, kick or block they were also focusing on driving these actions with the fundamentals of karate. Today, many senseis ignore this focus on the fundamentals to the detriment of their students. One of the reasons why karate masters who are over 80 years old are still able to perform almost superhuman feats of strength and power is because they have learned to master these basics of movement.

Moving Forward and Backward

When moving forward the karateka needs to put all the basics into practice plus add the following:

- All forward and backward movement begins with opening the stationary foot, the foot towards which the movement is being made, by 45 degrees.

- The mobile foot, the foot following the direction of the movement, must not only move in the required direction but also follow a semi-circular path towards the stationary foot. The reason for this movement is two fold, first, it ensures that the karateka does not move the body up and then down, and thus lose some forward momentum upwards, but instead drives the body forward with maximum force. Second, it ensures that the karateka keeps the leg movement within the body's optimum dimensions thus making it difficult for an opponent to break the balance of the karateka.

Starting position.

Starting position of the foot.

Turn the foot outward by 45 degrees.

Move the right foot on a semi-circular path to bring the feet together.

Take a step forward.

Moving forward—starting position.

Turning the back foot.

The feet together.

The step forward.

Turning and Changing Direction

As with forward and backward movement, sideways and direction changing movement needs to apply all the basics of movement. To this is added one more aspect. Always pivot on the heel and not the ball of the foot. This ensures that, at the completion of the turn or direction change, the body has moved a foot-length closer to the target than it would have if the pivot were done on the ball of the foot.

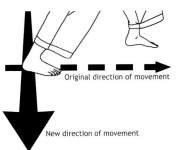
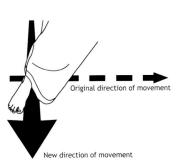
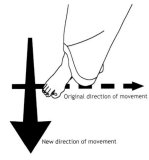

The starting position.

Turn on the heel.

Improper ball-of-the-foot turn leaves you short of your target.

BLOCKS

Blocks deflect an opponent's attack and they require skill and much practice to implement correctly. Remember that a block is not a head-on collision where only the strongest will win. A light block should be able to deflect the most powerful strike.

Five Important Points to Remember When Blocking

Practice these points with every block. When performing repetitive blocks in the dojo focus on performing all five of these points with every block.

- A block must be applied in the same manner as a strike, with your body and focus, your *ki*, maximized at the point of impact.

- A block should hurt your opponent but not hurt you. The point of impact of a block should be on the defender's hard point and the attacker's pressure point.

- Do not over-block. Block only within your body space so that you do not create an opening in your defense and allow your opponent to attack again. Below is an example of how an *uchi-uke* should and shouldn't be done. The pictures show the arms final position on completing the block.

Incorrect overblock.

Correct blocking technique.

Incorrect underblock.

- Twist the wrist on impact. This adds a great deal of extra force to the block and allows the block to be very strong and effective even if the forearm swings over a short distance.

- There is a certain angle at which the forearm can be bent to maximize the strength of a block. Never forget that a block will only be part of a series of moves involved in a fight and that the block may only be the first of many moves that the defender makes. To ensure that the defender is able to contend effectively with all other movements made by either the attacker or the defender himself, it is necessary to make use of these angles. The optimum angle is shown in the middle, below.

Incorrect blocking—too close.

Correct blocking technique.

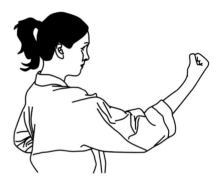

Incorrect blocking—too far.

TYPES OF BLOCKS

Gedan-uke (Downward Block)

This block is used to protect the lower torso and groin areas. The block should never extend past the upper leg and lower torso, or, in other words it should end with the outer arm being parallel to the body and leg on the same side as the blocking arm. Any block past this point will place the defender off balance. The blocking arm should also be at an angle of about 40 degrees from the body, or, if performed in *zenkutsu-dachi,* the completed block should see the fist of the blocking arm one fist-width above the forward leg.

*Diagram of a **gedan-uke** block.*

Two other views of the **gedan-uke** block.

Demonstration of a **gedan-uke** block.

Age-uke (Rising Block)

This block is used to defend the face and head from a direct punch or a downward swipe respectively. For maximum effect, strength, and balance, the forearm should not go beyond a 45-degree angle from the horizontal and should be no closer than a fist-width from the head. In addition the point of contact between the forearm and the attacker's weapon or arm must not go higher than the top of the defender's head. When performing the block the blocking arm must travel across the front of the chest and past the face.

Diagram of an **age-uke** block.

Demonstration of an **age-uke** block.

Age-uke *block in action.*

*Incorrect **age-uke** block—too close to head.*

*Incorrect **age-uke** block—too far from head.*

*An incorrectly applied **age-uke** block allows the opponent to unbalance the defender.*

Uchi-uke (Inside Block)

This block is one of two blocks used to defend the upper torso and neck areas. This is the weaker of the two blocks but often the first to respond as it is mostly performed by the defender's front-most arm. The block starts on the inside of the body area and blocks towards the outside. The block should never extend past the shoulder, and on completion, the forearm must be slightly bent away from the body.

Diagram of an **age-uke** *block.*

Demonstration of an **uchi-uke** *block.*

Soto-uke (Outside Block)

This block is the second of two blocks used to defend the upper torso and neck areas. This is the stronger of the two blocks. The block starts outside of the body area and blocks towards the inside extending towards the opposite outside of the body area. The block should never extend past the shoulder, and on completion, the forearm must be slightly bent away from the body.

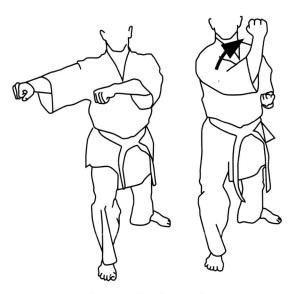

Diagram of a **soto-uke** *block.*

Demonstration of a **soto-uke** *block.*

Shuto-uke-gedan (Knife-Hand Block)

This is an open-handed block and operates in the same manner as the *gedan-uke* or *uchi-uke* depending on the area being protected. An advantage of blocking with an open hand means that the defender can grab onto the attacker's limb while in the process of blocking and then pull the opponent of balance.

Diagram of a **shuto-uke-gedan** *block.*

Demonstration of a **shuto-uke-gedan** *block.*

Juji-uke-chudan (Cross Block)

This block can be used to defend both the groin if blocking low or the head and face if blocking high. Where as all the other blocks deflect the attack this block brings the attack to a standstill. It is used against the *mae-geri* or against an attacker's downward swipe with a weapon towards the head. This block is fraught with danger, as the attacker will break the block and the defenders arms, if the attack is strong and the weapon hard or sharp.

Diagram of a **juji-uke-chudan** *block.*

Demonstration of a **juji-uke-chudan** *block.*

The **chudan-gyaka-zuki** *punch.*

CHAPTER 5

STRIKES AND KICKS

SPEED AND ACCURACY

Speed and accuracy complement each other, and cannot be separated. Hitting a moving target accurately can only be achieved with speedy actions or reactions. Continuous training of each movement improves muscle memory and ultimately improves the speed of the movement. On a more advanced level, having a thorough knowledge of the human body allows a karateka to aim at more specific targets, and, after years of practice, reliably strike them as they present themselves. This automatic response to presented targets further increases a karateka's speed. Of course, great speed and accuracy take lots of practice, and becomes most effective when in a state of *mushin*.

A sensei will usually instruct students to punch, block or kick to one of three areas:
- Head—*Jodan*
- Torso—*Chudan*
- Groin and legs—*Gedan*

These are taught to beginners but as karateka progress through their belts they must be taught to aim at specific pressure points on the head, torso and lower body.

STRIKES

The three most common methods of striking are with the fist, the elbow, and the open hand. It is vital that karateka practice striking solid objects such as punching bags, *makiwara*, jab pads and wooden dummies. By practicing on these training aids a karateka will soon realize the importance of making a proper fist—if the fist and wrist are not used correctly, the karateka will break one or the other. Also, remember that an opponent is not going to let you strike without attempting to block your strike—it is essential that the hands are sufficiently conditioned to withstand the rigors of combat.

Making a Fist

When making a fist, ensure that all the fingers fold into the palm with the thumb folded on the inside of the fist over the index and middle fingers. Keep the fist tightly clenched when striking. The tips of the fingers should fit snugly inside the palm of the hand and not be pinched. It they are, they will break during a punch. Long fingernails will cut the inside of the hand and so must be kept short.

Proper technique for making a fist.

Impact

All strikes must be fast and efficient. Follow the minimum distance between your hand and the target with a slight twist on impact that will lock your wrist and hand in an unbreakable position. A perfect strike ensures that all your body and focus, your *ki*, is maximized at the point of impact. Moving the non-striking hand in the opposite direction to the striking hand increases the speed of a strike.

Whichever strike you use, it is very important to remember to strike the target in a manner that will ensure that the jolt from the point of impact runs straight through your wrist and up your forearm. Should this not happen you will break your hand and/or wrist.

Lower Three-Knuckle Punch

This punch originates from a low level and is directed at an opponent's groin and stomach. The general direction of movement is upwards with the base at the thumb facing upwards. The wrist is locked in a position where the bottom of the fist and forearm create a single flat surface.

Two-Foreknuckle Punch

This punch is used for straight punching to an opponent's solar plexus, chest, neck and face. The base of the thumb faces to the side. The wrist is locked in a position where the top of the hand and the forearm create a single flat surface.

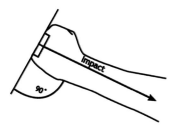 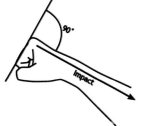 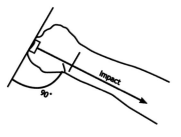

The mechanics of proper punches.

Hand Strikes

There are many ways that the hands and elbows may be used as a weapon. Finger strikes (*nukite, gyaku, washide, ippon yubi,* and *nihon yubi*) are effective on two of the most sensitive pressure points: the throat and eyes. The elbow strike (*hiji*) and knuckle strikes (*seiken* and *uraken*), using the middle and index fingers, are necessary when punching a hard target such as an opponent's chin, temple, sternum, or spine. Single knuckle strikes (*haito, ippon-ken-zuki* and *chudan-ken-zuki*) or multiple knuckle strike (*hiraken*) are very effective on pressure points on the side of the neck, arms, legs, torso, and back. The heel of the palm strike (*shotei* and *shuto*) is effective against the ribs, the nose, the collarbone, and joints. The base of the fist strike (*tettsui*) can provide a stunning blow to the top of the head, the shoulder, the kidneys, and the neck. The wrist strike (*ko-uchi*) can be used to surprise and affect an opponent's chin and the pressure points under an opponent's extended arm.

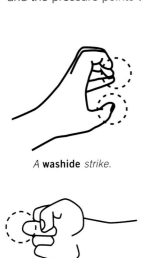

A **washide** *strike.*

A **hiji** *strike.*

A **chudan-ken-zuki** *strike.*

An **ippon-ken-zuki** *strike.*

A **haito** *strike.*

A **hiraken** *strike.*

Demonstration of a **chudan-hiji-zuki** *strike.*

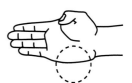

A **shotei** *strike.*

A **nukite** *strike.*

A **seiken** *strike.*

A **shuto** *strike.*

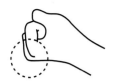

An **uraken** *strike.*   *A* **tettsui** *strike.*   *A* **gyaku** *strike.*   *An* **ippon yubi** *strike.*

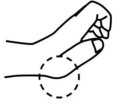

A **nyon yubi** *strike.*   *A* **teisho** *strike.*   *A* **ko-uchi** *strike.*

An example of a **washide** *strike on pressure points.*

Types of Fist and Elbow Strikes

The type of punch or strike used depends on the angle of attack, proximity to the opponent, and the particular pressure point to be struck. *Oi-zuki* and *gyaka-zuki* is used for distance strikes while *hiji* and *gakei* strikes are used for close-quarters fighting.

An **oi-zuki** *punch.*

A **tate-gyaka-zuki** *punch.*

A **chuden-zuki** *punch.*

A **gakei-zuki** *strike.*

A **hiji-zuki-chudan** *strike.*

A **hiji-zuki-jodan** *strike.*

Demonstration of a
jodan-gyaka-zuki *punch.*

Demonstration of a
gedan-gyaka-zuki *punch.*

Demonstration of a
chudan-gyaka-zuki *punch.*

Demonstration of a
jodan-oi-zuki *punch.*

Demonstration of a
chudan-oi-zuki *punch.*

Demonstration of a
gedan-oi-zuki *punch.*

KICKS

Kicks are the most powerful form of attack, but are generally slower to reach their target than strikes. The distance from an attacker's hand to an opponent's head is far shorter than the distance from the attacker's foot to the opponent's head. In addition, kicks generally work against gravity while punches, particularly lower punches, are assisted by gravity.

The consequences of a poor kick are far greater than a poor punch. A poor kick will place your legs far outside of the body's optimal dimension, leaving the attacker well off balance and vulnerable to a counterattack. Kicking should only be used when the art of kicking has been mastered and this mastery takes many years of practice.

Points of Contact

The top and side of the foot are full of sensitive bones and must be used with care. Always ensure that these parts of the foot (*haisoku*, *sokuto*, and *sokko*) are only used against targets that are softer, such as the neck, back, thigh, ribs, jaw, groin, and so forth, and not against the skull, forearm, or shin of an opponent. The heel (*kakato*) is very tough and

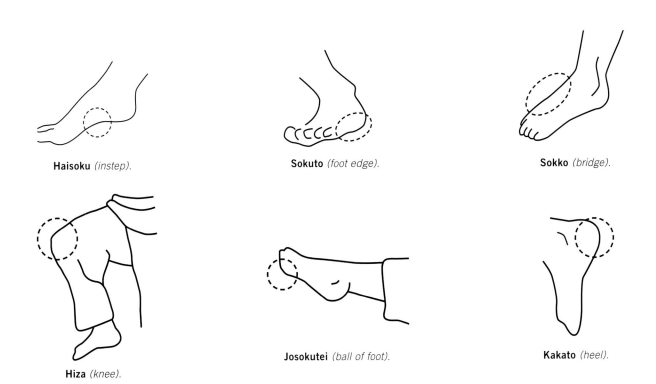

Haisoku *(instep).*

Sokuto *(foot edge).*

Sokko *(bridge).*

Hiza *(knee).*

Josokutei *(ball of foot).*

Kakato *(heel).*

can be used effectively against almost any part of an opponent. The ball of the foot, when used effectively, is also very strong. The knee (*hiza*) is strong but inflexible except in close-in fighting. Beware of the pressure points on the side of the knee as a bump on these can cause incapacitation to the entire leg.

A **mae-geri** *kick.*

A **mawashi-geri** *kick.*

A **mikazuki-geri** *kick.*

A **kakato otashi-geri** *kick.*

An **ushiro-mawashi-geri** *kick.*

A **hiza-geri** *kick.*

A **yoko-geri** *kick.*

An **ushiro-geri** *kick.*

Demonstration of a **mae-geri** *kick.*

Demonstration of a **jodan-mawashi-geri** *kick.*

Demonstration of an **ushiro-geri** *kick.*

Demonstration of a **yoko-geri** *kick.*

Types of Kicks

With the exeption of the *hiza-geri*, all other kicks are for distance fighting. Kicks must only be used when the speed and accuracy of kicks is as good as that of the arms and hands. Kicks are much stronger than strikes but, to the untrained, much slower and less accurate.

Kicking Methods

There are two ways in which a karateka can kick, namely a *kekomi* (thrust) kick and a *keage* (snap) kick. They are both effective but are used in different circumstances.

The *kekomi* will have a greater impact on the target and will almost certainly destabilize and do damage to the defender. The disadvantage of a *kekomi* kick is that it extends outside the body's optimal dimensions resulting in the attacker losing balance forward. Another disadvantage of the *kekomi* kick is that the defender has more time to grab the attacker's leg and then counterattack. These types of kicks may be applied to *yoko*, *mawashi* and *mae-geris*. A *kekomi* kick is generally used by a karateka when an opponent has committed themselves to an attack from which they cannot withdraw, an example being a lunge punch where the opponent lifts their front foot clear off the ground and is unable to alter or modify this movement before the landing the front foot. The karateka can then give total commitment to the *kekomi* kick.

The *keagi* is a very quick kick, a snap kick, and is performed within the body's optimal dimensions. It is generally used when in close contact with a defender. The *keagi* is also used when the attacker delivers a combination of attacks as the *keagi* allows the attacker to maintain balance even if the kick is blocked or misses.

Aiming a **mae-geri** *kick with the knee.*

Aiming a **mawashi-geri** *kick with the knee.*

Aiming of Kicks

All kicks are aimed through the knee. This does not mean that the knee will always point directly at the target, in fact, this only occurs with a few kicks, but for any kick to be effective the knee must be aimed, raised, and released correctly. This takes much practice. The aiming point of the knee may vary from style to style for exactly the same kick.

Foot Position

The direction the non-kicking foot points determines the strength and power behind each kick.

In the case of a *mae-geri*, *hanshis* from different styles will teach different positions, all of which provide a great deal of power. The two most common positions for a non-kicking foot are:
- Pointed directly at the target.
- Angled 45 degrees away from the target when kicking.

In the case of the foot pointing directly at the target the kick is made more powerful by launching the hips into the target and thus the full body weight into the kick. By angling the foot at 45 degrees the karateka is able to kick further, or deeper into the target. Both these methods result in much the same power.

Mawashi-geris are made more effective through greater rotation of the non-kicking foot. In addition, by rotating on the ball of the foot, the reach of the kicking leg is also greater. A foot that swivels through 90 degrees has less power and reach than a foot that swivels through 180 degrees. By positioning the non-kicking foot at 180 degrees the kicking leg is able to use the full weight of the body to kick "through" the target with out losing balance. The same principle applies to *ushiro-mawashi-geri*. In addition, by rotating through 180 degrees, a karateka can kick higher with a *mawashi-geri* and *ushiro-geri*.

A *yoko-geri* can be a very powerful kick but only if the non-kicking foot rotates through 180 degrees. Isaac Newton's theory that states "For every action there is an equal and opposite reaction" is very important. A kick releases enormous force in one direction and it is only through correct foot position that the equal and opposite force is absorbed by the body of the kicker with out causing the kicker to overcorrect and lose balance.

The foot of the standing leg points in the opposite direction to the target for effective **yoko-geri** *and* **mawashi-geri**.

This pectoralis and biceps stretch is described on page 70.

CHAPTER 6

WARM-UP AND STRETCHING

PREPARATION FOR TRAINING

Karate, more so than most other sports, requires that its participants be physically well-prepared for their training. The reason for this lays in the nature of karate, which requires rapid acceleration and deceleration from muscles, high impact on muscles and joints and aggressive use of the joints and ligaments.

Many karate classes dedicate a lot of time, up to 25% of the total class time, to warming up. Although this is not a waste of time it does reduce the amount of time that can be actively spent on training. The warm-up and stretching exercises that follow combine the preparation of muscles, joints and ligaments with basic training. By the time the warm-up is complete the students will have performed most of the stances, strikes and kicks. A common mistake among physical trainers is that they tend to stretch before the muscles are warmed-up. Muscles should only be stretched once blood has circulated through them. Cold muscles should never be stretched.

A warm-up should be done for at least five to ten minutes at a low intensity, at about 50–60% of the maximum heart rate. After these exercises your muscles should be warm—only then should you stretch the primary muscles.

The cool down is similar to the warm-up in that it should last five to ten minutes and be done at a low intensity (50–60% of max heart rate). After you have completed your training and cooled-down properly, it is then important that you stretch the primary muscles that have been used. Warming-up, stretching, and cooling-down are very important to every exercise session. They not only help your performance levels and produce better results, but they also drastically decrease your risk of injury.

ACTIVATING THE CORE MUSCLES

An important part of any martial art is the *ki*, the vital power that flows from your body. Ki does have a physical source, and is not some mystical, other-worldly phenomenon. Physiotherapists and other anatomically knowledgeable individuals term the muscles that produce this power the Core Muscles or the Stabilizing Muscles. Certain martial arts term the area that generates the *ki* the *hara* or *tan den*. Using these muscles effectively takes much training but once used properly they will insure that an individual's karate becomes extremely effective and efficient. Strong core muscles will strengthen the spine and provide a solid foundation for the use of the limbs.

Exercises that strengthen the core muscles.

The core muscles work together as a coordinated group and consist of:

- *Transversus abdominus*—a horizontally orientated muscle lying beneath the other abdominal muscles.
- *Multifidi*—small muscles at the back of the spine that connect the spinal segments together.
- *Pelvic Floor*—forms the base of the stabilizing muscles of the abdomen.
- *Diaphragm*—forms the top of the stabilizing muscles of the abdomen.

The stabilizing muscles should be activated during all movement to attain overall stabilization of the body. To do this the spine must be in a neutral position and normal breathing must be maintained. To exercise, pull the muscles below the belly button towards your spine and lift the pelvic muscle (do this while breathing normally). To warm up the core muscles adopt the positions shown above and hold them for a count of twenty. Hold the lower stance on both the right and left arm.

WARM-UP

The warm up should begin with exercises involving your whole body, and should last for about five to ten minutes, depending on the temperature. The aim of this phase is to:

- Raise the temperature of your muscles
- Increase the amount of blood flowing to your muscles
- Raise the temperature of your body

You should be sweating lightly at the end of this phase and your pulse rate should have risen to about 120 beats per minute before moving onto the next phase.

Remember, the first minute is as important as the last minute.

ACTIVITY 1 **_Heisoku_**—Move up and down on ball of foot.

DURATION Ten counts

MUSCLES Calves and achilles tendon

ACTIVITY 2 **_Heiko_**—Move up and down on ball of foot.

DURATION Ten counts

MUSCLES Calves and achilles tendon

ACTIVITY 3 **_Kiba_**—Back straight, up and down on ball of foot.

DURATION Ten counts

MUSCLES Calves and achilles tendon

ACTIVITY 4 **_Shiko_**—Grab bottom of _gi_ pants, alternate up and down movement on ball of feet. Left up, right down and vice versa .

DURATION Ten counts

MUSCLES Calves and achilles tendon

ACTIVITY 5 Slow jog around the dojo.

DURATION One circuit

MUSCLES Lower body

ACTIVITY 6 Stop, and swing the arms forward.

DURATION Ten counts

MUSCLES Loosening up rotator cuff and warming shoulder

	DURATION	MUSCLES
ACTIVITY 7 Medium speed jog around dojo, kicking backward.	One circuit	Lower body
ACTIVITY 8 Stop, and swing the arms backward.	Ten counts	Loosening up rotator cuff and warming shoulder
ACTIVITY 9 Medium speed jog around dojo, kicking backward (see diagram on opposite page).	One circuit	Hamstring and inner thigh
ACTIVITY 10 Stop, and swing one arm forward and one arm backward.	Ten counts	Shoulders
ACTIVITY 11 Medium speed jog around dojo, lifting the knees (see diagram on opposite page).	One circuit	Quads and hipflexors

	DURATION	MUSCLES
ACTIVITY 12 Stop, ten push-ups (on fingers, knuckles, or hands, depending on individual strength).	Ten counts	Chest and triceps
ACTIVITY 13 Fast run around dojo. knuckles or hands depending on individual strength)	One circuit	Full body

ACTIVITY 14 Stop, ten situps.
DURATION Ten counts
MUSCLES Abdominals

ACTIVITY 15 Fast run around dojo.
DURATION One circuit
MUSCLES Full body

ACTIVITY 16 Stop, ten punches at maximum speed.
DURATION Ten counts
MUSCLES Overall upper body

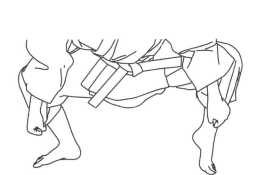

Shiko—*Grab bottom of gi pants, alternate up and down movement on ball of feet. Left up, right down, and vice versa*

Medium speed jog around dojo kicking backward.

Medium speed jog around dojo lifting the knees.

STRETCHING

You should stretch those parts of your body that will be used during your match or training session. Hold each stretch for ten seconds at the point of slight discomfort, and remember to relax. Never stretch cold muscles, and *don't bounce*.

Part 1—Legs

STANCE **Shiko**

ACTION Back straight, arms stretched out in front.

MUSCLES Quadriceps

STANCE **Hachiji**

ACTION Bend, touch the floor with legs straight.

MUSCLES Hamstring and lower back

STANCE **Nahanchi**

ACTION Bend, touch the floor with legs straight.

MUSCLES Hamstring and lower back

STANCE **Heiku**   ACTION Bend, grab ankles.   MUSCLES Hamstring

STANCE **Nahanchi**
ACTION Bend, grab left and then right ankle.
MUSCLES Hamstring

STANCE **Masuba**
ACTION Bend, touch the floor.
MUSCLES Hamstring stretch

STANCE **Zenkutsu** (left and right)
ACTION Lower stance with each count.
MUSCLES Quadriceps and hipflexors

STANCE **Nekoashi** (left and right)
ACTION Lower stance with each count.
MUSCLES Tendon and calves

STANCE **Kosa** (left and right)
ACTION Lower stance with each count.
MUSCLES Achilles tendon

WARM-UP AND STRETCHING **69**

ACTIVITY	ACTION	MUSCLES
Center split	Lower with each count.	Hamstrings
Center split with pelvis forward	Hold.	Hamstrings, abdominals, hipflexors, and back

ACTIVITY Supine gluteal stretch

ACTION Lie on back. Cross left leg over right and pull back on left leg. Then cross right leg over left and pull back on the right leg.

MUSCLES Gluteals

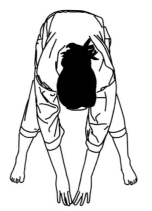

The above diagrams show how the **Shiko***,* **Hachiji***,* **Heiku** *and* **Nahanchi** *stretches are performed.*

Part 2—Upper Body and Neck

ACTION Waist twist clockwise then counter-clockwise (five counts each direction).
MUSCLES Obliques

ACTION Upper body twist.
MUSCLES Obliques

ACTION Look left then right (see diagram on opposite page).
MUSCLES Neck

ACTION Roll head from left to right.
MUSCLES Neck

ACTION With a partner push left arms against each other with elbow bent.
MUSCLES Pectoralis

ACTION With a partner push right arms against each other with elbow bent.
MUSCLES Pectoralis

ACTION With a partner push left arms against each other with elbow straight.
MUSCLES Pectoralis and biceps

ACTION With a partner push right arms against each other with elbow straight.
MUSCLES Pectoralis and biceps

ACTION Lie on back, knees pulled upward toward chest, drop over to side (see right diagram below).
MUSCLES Lower back

ACTION Hanging stretch—between shoulder blades.
MUSCLES Trapezius and latisimus

Look left, then right.

Lie on back, pull knees upward toward chest, and drop them over to one side, then the other.

Part 3—Arms, Wrists, and Shoulders

ACTION Left arm across the body, right arm hugging left arm close to body.
MUSCLES Shoulders

ACTION Right arm across body, left arm hugging right arm close to body (see diagram 1 on page 74).
MUSCLES Shoulders

ACTION Left arm raised with right arm pulling on left elbow toward the rear.
MUSCLES Triceps

ACTION Right arm raised with left arm pulling on right elbow toward the rear (see diagram 2 on page 74).
MUSCLES Triceps

ACTION Extend left arm to the front, keep arm straight, clasp the left hand with the right hand and pull the left hand up into a vertical position (see diagram 3 on page 74).
MUSCLES Forearm flexors (Inside of arm)

ACTION Extend right arm to the front, keep arm straight, clasp the right hand with the left hand and pull the right hand up into a vertical position.
MUSCLES Forearm flexors (Inside of arm)

ACTION Extend left arm to the front, keep arm straight, clasp the left hand with the right hand and pull the left hand down into a vertical position (see diagram 5 on page 74).
MUSCLES Forearm extensors (top/upside)

ACTION Extend right arm to the front, keep arm straight, clasp the right hand with the left hand and pull the right hand down into a vertical position.
MUSCLES Forearm extensors (top/upside)

ACTION Put arms behind back, bend forward and face palms upward (see diagram 4 on page 74).
MUSCLES Shoulders and pectoratis

ACTION Flick both wrists up and down.
MUSCLES Extensiors and abductors

ACTION Flick both wrists from side to side.
MUSCLES Extensiors and abductors

ACTION Cross the right arm under the left, clasp hands, and look over the right shoulder.
MUSCLES Neck

ACTION Cross the left arm under the right, clasp hands, and look over the left shoulder.
MUSCLES Neck

Diagram 1. Right arm across body, left arm hugging right arm close to body.

Diagram 2. Left arm raised with right arm pulling on left elbow toward the rear.

Diagram 3. Extend left arm to the front, keep arm straight, clasp the left hand with the right hand and pull the left hand up into a vertical position.

Diagram 4. Put arms behind back, bend forward and face palms upward.

Diagram 5. Cross the right arm under the left clasp hands and look over the right shoulder.

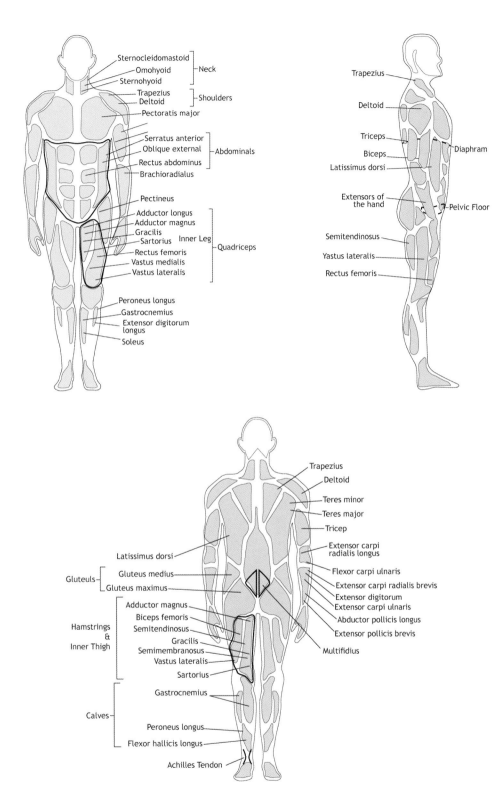

The major muscle and muscle groups of the human body are shown in these diagrams and relate to the exercises and stretches.

Geri waza *(page 81).*

CHAPTER 7

TRAINING EXERCISES

In this phase, which should last for about five minutes, the aim is to get ready for the task ahead by performing exercises that are directly related to the effort to be made, be it a match, training, or taking a test.

You should include:
- Bursts of fast and slow exercises
- Twists and changes in direction

Blocks, Strikes and Kicks (Junior Level)

Kihon Uke

Begin in *yoi* position. Beginning with left hand moving to *age*, then right hand to *soto*, left to *gedaan barai*, right to *uchi*, left to *shuto*. Repeat process beginning with right hand.

Kihon uke: *begin.*   **Kihon uke:** *step 1.*

Kihon Uke (continued)

Kihon uke: *step 2.*

Kihon uke: *step 3.*

Kihon uke: *step 4.*

Kihon uke: *step 5.*

Kihon uke: *end.*

Kihon Zuki

Begin in *yoi* position. Begin with left hand punching to *chuden* with a *kia*. Then *jodan, chudan* and *gedan*. Repeat.

Kihon zuke: *begin.*

Kihon zuke: *step 1.*

Kihon zuke: *step 2.*

Kihon zuke: *step 3.*

Kihon zuke: *end.*

Kihon Geri

Begin in *yoi* and move into fighting stance with a *kiai*. Begin with left leg *mae geri chudan kekomi* (5 repetitions), change stance to left leg forward and do five reps of right leg *mae geri chudan kekomi*. Change stance to right leg forward with five reps of *mawashi geri chudan*. Change stance to left leg forward with five reps of *mawashi geri chudan*. Change stance to right leg forward with five reps of *yoko geri chudan kekomi*. Change stance to left leg forward with five reps of *yoko geri chudan kekomi*.

Kihon geri: *Begin.*

Kihon geri: *step 1.*

Kihon geri: *step 2.*

Kihon geri: *step 3.*

Kihon geri: *step 4.*

Kihon geri: *end.*

Blocks, Strikes and Kicks (Senior Level)

Geri Waza

Begin in *yoi* position. Kick with left leg to *mae geri chudan, yoko geri chudan, ushuro geri judan* and return to *yoi*. Move to *zenkutsu dachi* with left leg back. Kick *mawasi geri chudan* with left leg and return left leg to *zenkutsu dachi*. Return to *yoi*. Repeat with right leg. *Kia* after *mawashi-geri*.

Geri waza: *begin.*

Geri waza: *step 1.*

Geri waza: *step 2.*

Geri waza: *step 3.*

Geri waza: *step 4.*

Geri waza: *step 5.*

Geri waza: *step 6.* **Geri waza:** *step 7.* **Geri waza:** *end.*

Shuto Waza

Begin in *yoi*. Striking first right and then left begin with a *shuto uchi mawasi jodan*, then *shuto uke jodan, nukite uchi jodan, shuto uchi sakotsu, haitto uchi jodan, haitto uchi jodan* (other hand), step back with right leg and *juji uke*, step forward with right leg and *shuto uchi mawasi jodan* with both hands. Front leg back to *yoi*. Repeat starting with left hand.

The sequence of steps in **Shuto Waza.** *The first five movements are done to the left and the right.*

Shuto waza: *begin.*

Shuto waza: *step 1.*

Shuto waza: *step 2.*

Shuto waza: *step 3.*

Shuto waza: *step 4.*

Shuto waza: *step 5.*

Shuto waza: *step 6.*

Shuto waza: *step 7.*

Shuto waza: *end.*

Juppo Geri Undo

Stand in the *yoi* position, and, with each kick, move forward into *kamae*. Kick with alternating legs, starting with the left. Perform the following kicks: *hittsui, mae geri gedan, mae geri chudan, mae geri jodan, yoko geri gedan, yoko geri chudan, yoko geri jodan, mawasi geri chudan, mawasi geri jodan, ushuro geri chudan*. Turn and repeat sequence, starting on right leg.

Juppo geri undo: *begin.*

Juppo geri undo: *step 1.*

Juppo geri undo: *step 2.*

Juppo geri undo: *step 3.*

Juppo geri undo: *step 4.*

Juppo geri undo: *step 5.*

Juppo geri undo: *step 6.*

Juppo geri undo: *step 7.*

Juppo geri undo: *step 8.*

Juppo geri undo: *step 9.*

Juppo geri undo: *end.*

Yotsukado no Renshu

Each drill has fourteen steps, and each step has two moves. The first move is a block, and the second move is a strike. There are two *kiais* in the drill. The first *kiai* is at the strike on step 7 and the second is at the strike on the final step, step fourteen. Each step is either a turn through 90 degrees, or 180 degrees to the open side of the stance. In the example below the block is a *geden berei,* and the strike is a *chudan zuki*.

Start by standing in *yoi*. On the command to start, look to the right before taking the first step.

Step 90 degrees to the left into *zenkutsu dachi*, using your left leg, with a *gedan berei* and then *chudan zuki;* repeat the sequence, stepping 90 degrees to your right, using your right leg; step 180 degrees to your left; step 90 degrees to your right; step 180 degrees to your left; step 90 degrees to your right; step 180 degrees to your left and *kiai* on the punch.

That was the first half, now you are going to repeat the whole sequence but this time you start from the right hand side.

Step 90 degrees to the right into *zenkutsu dachi,* using your right leg, with a *gedan berei* and then *chudan zuki;* repeat the sequence, stepping 90 degrees to the left, using your left leg; step 180 degrees to your right; step 90 degrees to your left; step 180 degrees to your right; step 90 degrees to your left; step 180 degrees to your right and *kiai* on the punch.

Begin in the **yoi** *stance and, on the start command, look to the left before stepping.*

After stepping, the first move is always a block over the leg that has moved. The block can be a **gedan berei,** *as shown, or any other block.*

After the block, the second move is a strike. The strike can be a **chudan zuki,** *or it can be any other strike.*

Yotsukado no renshu: *begin.*

Yotsukado no renshu: *step 1, move 1.*

Yotsukado no renshu: step 2.

Yotsukado no renshu: step 1, move 2.

Yotsukado no renshu: step 3.

Yotsukado no renshu: step 4.

Yotsukado no renshu: *step 6.*

Yotsukado no renshu: *step 5.*

Yotsukado no renshu: *step 7 and* kiai.

Yotsukado no renshu: *step 8.*

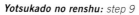

Yotsukado no renshu: step 9

Yotsukado no renshu: step 10.

Yotsukado no renshu: step 11.

Yotsukado no renshu: step 12.

Yotsukado no renshu: step 13.　　*Yotsukado no renshu:* step 14 and kiai.

Yotsukado no renshu: end.

WARM DOWN

At the end of a warm up you should feel warm rather than hot and be slightly out of breath. If your warm up is in preparation for a match you should aim to complete warming up ten to fifteen minutes prior to the start of the game. Return to the dressing room and keep warm. If you are warming up to train, then off you go.

Warming down is just as vital as warming up. The objective is to return the body gradually to its resting state. This can be done by slowly decreasing the intensity of the training in the last ten minutes of the class or by having a specific warm down session. This helps to prevent muscle stiffness and the onset of muscle soreness that can follow a particularly hard match or training session.

One method of performing a warm down is to perform at least one of the stretching exercises per main muscle group: chest, back, hamstings, quadriceps, and calves.

*Signature move of **Kusanka Dai***

CHAPTER 8

KATA ORIGINS

KARATE TRAINING TOOLS

Kata are a compilation of individual techniques put into sequences in which a karateka encounters one or more imaginary opponents. All the strikes, kicks, stances and blocks that a karateka gets taught are brought together in the various kata. Usually, as a student is taught new techniques he will be taught a kata that incorporates these techniques.

The basic katas of *Shotokan*, *Wado-ryu,* and *Shorin-ryu,* namely the *Pinan* or *Heian* katas, have five levels (*Shodan* to *Godan)* that become increasingly more complex. Some of the more advanced katas such as the *Passai* or *Bassai* katas come in minor, *sho,* and major, *dai,* versions. The major version usually being more complex than the minor version.

A number of kata have names that are translated into numbers such as 13, 18, 24, 36, 54 and 108. In many cases these numbers reflect the number of moves in the kata but they are also very important numbers in Buddhist mythology and thus have a deeper meaning. *Bunkai* is the practical application of a kata and shows how the kata is used to attack and defend against the imaginary opponents. It is important that students understand the *bunkai* as it will assist them in improving their kata.

Certain kata, known by the same name, are used by a number of different karate styles but will vary in technique from style to style. In fact, in extreme instances, the katas may vary in stances, strikes and even the number and formation of the movements so that the kata is completely different. It is for this reason that WKF competitions do not have a single kata event but instead have events for each of the four main karate styles. Thus a *Wado-ryu* competitor who chooses to do *Chinto* as one of his competition katas will only compete against other *Wado-ryu* competitors and not against *Shotokan* or *Shito-ryu* competitors who may also be doing *Chinto.*

When Gichin Funakoshi brought karate to Japan in the early 1900s Japan and China were at war and anti-Chinese sentiment in Japan was high. Many of the kata that Funakoshi brought with him from Okinawa had Chinese names and, in order to market his style better, he changed the names of these Okinawan kata to Japanese. An example is *Chinto,* so known in *Wado-ryu* and *Shorin-ryu,* which he changed to *Gankaku* as it is now known in *Shotokan.*

Goju-ryu, unlike the other styles discussed in this book, has four groupings for its kata. These are *Kihongata,* which means "basic kata;" *Heishugata,* which means "closed hand kata" but also means "fundamental kata;" *Kaishugata,* which means "open hand kata;" and *Fukyugata,* which means "promotional kata." *Kihongata* are the simplest, followed by the intermediate kata of *Heishugata* and then the advanced kata of *Kaishugata.* The *Fukyugata* are not traditional *Goju-ryu* kata but were developed to promote karate in general.

ORIGINS OF THE DIFFERENT KATA

Bassai

See Passai

Chinte

Meaning: Unusual hand
Founder: No known founder
History: The kata originated in China and was brought to Okinawa by a Chinese martial artist.
Characteristics: An advanced kata
Also known as: No other name
Used by: *Shotokan*

Chinto

Meaning: Fighter to the East
Founder: Sokon Matsumura
History: Legend has it that *Chinto* was the nickname given to a Chinese sailor by the name of *Annan* who was shipwrecked on the Okinawan coast and who stole from the locals. When Sokon Matsumura went to deal with him he found that Annan was a very good fighter, at least as good as Matsumura himself. Matsumura then sought to learn from Annan and Matsumura developed the kata *Chinto* in honor of Annan.
Characteristics: An advanced and complex kata
Also known as: *Gankaku* in *Shotokan*, which means "crane on a rock"
Used by: *Shotokan*, *Shito-ryu*, *Shorin-ryu*

Signature move of **Chinto.**

Empi

See Wanshu

Gangaku

See Chinto

Gekisai *Dai Ichi*, *Ni* and *San*

Meaning: Attack and destroy
Founder: Chojun Miyagi
History: The kata was created by Miyagi after 1936 as a *Fukyu* kata.
Characteristics: The *Ichi* and *Ni* versions are fairly basic but the *San* (not practiced by all schools) is intermediate—a *Fukyugata*
Also known as: No other name
Used by: *Goju-ryu* and *Shorin-ryu* (*Matsubushi* school)

Gojushiho (some schools have a *Sho* and *Dai*)

Meaning: Fifty four steps
Founder: Sokon Matsumura
History: Based on a sequence used in *Kung-fu* that imitates the movements of a woodpecker.
Characteristics: An advanced kata
Also known as: No other name
Used by: *Shotokan*, *Shito-ryu*, *Wado-ryu* and *Shorin-ryu*

Gorin

Meaning: Five Rings
Founder: Shugoro Nakazato
History: Developed to commemorate the 1996 Atlanta Olympic Games.
Characteristics: An intermediate kata
Also known as: No other name
Used by: *Shorin-ryu* (*Shorinkan* school)

Hangetsu

See Seisan

Heian

See Pinan

Ji'in

Meaning: Love of truth
Founder: No known founder
History: Originated in the *Tomari-te* schools
Characteristics: An advanced kata
Also known as: No other name
Used by: *Shotokan*

Jion

Meaning: Temple Bells
Founder: No known founder
History: Originated from *Kempo* boxing and practiced by the *Tomari-te* schools.
Characteristics: An intermediate *kata*
Also known as: No other name
Used by: *Shotokan* and *Wado-ryu*

Jitte

Meaning: Ten hands
Founder: No known founder
History: Originated in the *Tomari-te* schools. There are a number of interpretations one of which is that the *bunkai* shows how to defend against ten opponents including attacks from a *bo* and another that the kata is in fact a *Kobudo* kata for *jitte*, a type of *sai*.
Characteristics: Advanced
Also known as: *Sip Soo*
Used by: *Shotokan*

Kanku

See Kusanku

Kihon

Meaning: Basic
Founder: Each style of martial art lists its own founder.
History: *Kihon* kata are used by many martial arts as they are the practice of the most basic movements of the martial art and are often the first kata taught to students. They have been redeveloped, changed and modified many times through out the development of martial arts.
Characteristics: Very basic kata
Also known as: *Tekki* in *Shotokan,* meaning "basic"
Used by: *Shotokan* and *Shorin-ryu*

Kururumfa

Meaning: Holding on long and striking suddenly
Founder: Chojun Miyagi
History: Based on the *Kung-fu* praying mantis style
Characteristics: An advanced kata—a *Kaishugata*
Also known as: No other name
Used by: *Wado-ryu*

Kusanku (*Sho* and *Dai*)

Meaning: Refers to a Chinese diplomat or military officer
Founder: Satunushi Sakugawa
History: Kusanku spent some time in Okinawa where he taught *Kempo* boxing. He is considered to be one of the major influences on karate. Sakugawa combined many of his techniques into a single kata that he called *Kusanku*. Sakugawa taught the kata to Matsumura who then broke it down into its major and minor forms.
Characteristics: Advanced kata which incorporates a jump
Also known as: *Kanku,* which means "gazing at the sky or heavens"
Used by: *Shotokan, Shito-ryu, Wado-ryu, Goju-ryu* and *Shorin-ryu*

Signature move of **Kusanka Sho.**

Meikyo

See Rohai

Naihanchi (*Shodan*, *Nidan* and *Sandan*)

Meaning: Defend your ground

Founder: Sokon Matsumura

History: Matsumura originally developed a single *Naihanchi* kata and it was Itosu who broke it down into *Shodan* and *Nidan*. Itosu then developed *Sandan*.

Characteristics: An Intermediate kata

Also known as: *Naifanchi*

Used by: *Shorin-ryu* and *Wado-ryu*

Signature move of **Nahanchi Shodan.**

Signature Move of **Nahanchi Nidan**.

Signature move of **Nahanchi Sandan.**

Neseishi

Meaning: Twenty-four steps

Founder: No known founder

History: It is believed that the kata originates from the *Kung-fu* dragon style.

Characteristics: An advanced kata

Also known as: *Nijushiho* in *Shotokan*

Used by: *Shotokan* and *Wado-ryu*

Nijushiho

See Neseishi

Passai (*Sho* and *Dai*)

Meaning: Penetrating the fortress

Founder: Sokon Matsumura

History: This kata has links to martial arts practiced in Korea and China and it is believed to have originated in various Chinese boxing and *Kung-fu* styles. This kata was also practiced by the *Tomari-te* schools.

Characteristics: An intermediate *kata*

Also known as: *Bassai* in *Shotokan*

Used by: *Shotokan*, *Shito-ryu*, *Wado-ryu,* and *Shorin-ryu*

Signature move of **Passai Sho.**

Signature move of **Pinan Shodan**.

Signature move of **Passai Dai**.

Signature move of **Pinan Nidan.**

Pinan (*Shodan, Nidan, Sandan, Yondan,* and *Godan*)
Meaning: Peaceful mind
Founder: Anko Itosu
History: Itosu developed these five relatively easy *kata* from the *Kusanku* and *Gojushiho* katas to teach school children the basics of karate.
Characteristics: A basic kata
Also known as: *Heian* in *Shotokan,* which means "long peace"
Used by: *Shotokan, Shito-ryu, Wado-ryu,* and *Shorin-ryu*

Signature move of **Pinan Sandan**.

Signature move of **Pinan Yondan**.

Signature move of **Pinan Godan**.

Rohai (*Shodan*, *Nidan*, and *Sandan*)
Meaning: Vision of a crane
Founder: Kosaku Matsumora
History: The kata was originally taught in the *Tomari-te* schools of karate. Anko Itosu later took the kata and developed it into three katas. Some styles practice all three *Rohai* kata and others just one *Rohai* kata.
Characteristics: An advanced kata
Also known as: *Meikyo* in *Shotokan*, which means "bright mirror"
Used by: *Shotokan*, *Shito-ryu*, *Wado-ryu,* and *Shorin-Ryu*.

Saifa
Meaning: Destroy and defeat
Founder: *Chojun Miyagi*
History: The kata was developed by Miyagi to teach how to throw an opponent and also how to defend against throws from one or more opponents.
Characteristics: An intermediate kata—a *Kaishugata*
Also known as: No other name
Used by: *Goju-ryu*

Sanchin

Meaning: "Three battles," but refers to the stance *Sanchin-dachi*

Founder: Chojun Miyagi

History: Developed by Miyagi to focus on *ki*

Characteristics: A basic kata—a *Kihongata* and a *Heishugata*

Also known as: No other name

Used by: *Goju-ryu*

Sanseiru

Meaning: Thirty-six hands

Founder: Chojun Miyagi

History: Developed by Miyagi to teach complex punching combinations as well as many entry and joint breaking techniques. It also teaches defense against kicks.

Characteristics: An advanced kata—a *Kaishugata*

Also known as: No other names

Used by: *Goju-ryu*

Seisan

Meaning: Thirteen hands

Founder: No known founder

History: A very old kata that originated with the *Naha-te* schools.

Characteristics: An advanced kata—a *Kaishugata*

Also known as: *Hangetsu* in *Shotokan*, meaning "half moon" in Japanese. *Seishan* in *Wado-ryu* also means "thirteen hands."

Used by: *Shotokan*, *Goju-ryu* and *Wado-ryu*

Seiunchin

Meaning: Attack, conquer, suppress

Founder: Chojun Miyagi

History: The kata was developed to focus on sweeps and other leg techniques, but not kicks.

Characteristics: An intermediate kata—a *Kaishugata*

Also known as: No other name

Used by: *Goju-ryu*

Sepai

Meaning: Eighteen hands

Founder: Chojun Miyagi

History: The kata was developed with a number of subtle and hidden moves that take some time to develop effectively.

Characteristics: An advanced kata—a *Kaishugata*

Also known as: No other name

Used by: *Goju-ryu*

Shisochin

Meaning: Destroy in four directions

Founder: Chojun Miyagi

History: Miyagi Chojun called *Shisochin* his favorite kata when he was growing old, as he believed it to be best suited to his body type at that time.

Characteristics: An intermediate to advanced kata—a *Kaishugata*

Also known as: No other name

Used by: *Goju-ryu*

Sochin

Meaning: Tranquil Force

Founder: Seisho Aragaki

History: Taught in the *Naha-te* schools and then passed on to *Shito-ryu*. Yoshitaka, Gichin Funakoshi's son introduced it to *Shotokan*.

Characteristics: An advanced kata

Also known as: no other name

Used by: *Shotokan* and *Shito-ryu*

Suparimpei

Meaning: One hundred and eight hands

Founder: Chojun Miyagi

History: Legend has it that this kata represented a band of 108 warriors that travelled the Chinese countryside in the 1600s, performing "Robin Hood"-type tasks, doing good deeds and giving to the poor.

Characteristics: A very advanced kata—a *Kaishugata*

Also known as: *Pechurrin* in Chinese and *haiko Hachi Ho* in *Shotokan*.

Used by: *Wado-ryu* and *Goju-ryu*

Taikyoku Shodan

Meaning: First course

Founder: Gichin Funakoshi

History: This kata was developed as a way to simplify the principles of the already simplified *Pinan/Heian* series.

Characteristics: A very basic kata

Also known as: No other name

Used by: *Shotokan* and *Goju-ryu* (five versions)

Tekki

See Kihon

Tensho

Meaning: Revolving hands

Founder: Chojun Miyagi

History: *Tensho* was created on 1921 as a softer version of *sanchin*.

Characteristics: An intermediate kata—a *Heishugata*

Also known as: *Rokkishu*

Used by: *Goju-ryu*

Unsu

Meaning: Cloud hands

Founder: No known founder

History: It is belived to have originated in the *Kung-fu* dragon style.

Characteristics: An advanced kata

Also known as: No other name

Used by: *Shotokan* and *Shito-ryu*

Wankan

Meaning: Emperor's crown

Founder: No known founder

History: A very old kata that was practiced by the *Tomari-te* schools.

Characteristics: An advanced kata

Also known as: No other name

Used by: *Shotokan* and *Shorin-ryu*

Wanshu

Meaning: Flying swallow

Founder: Sappushi Wang Ji, an official from Xiuning

History: Wang Ji, a practitioner of *Kempo* boxing, enjoyed throwing and jumping on his adversaries and these movements resembeled the flight of a swallow. Another theory is that this kata was a product of the interaction between Okinawans and the so-called "Thirty-six Chinese Families" that immigrated to the islands in the late 1300s. Yet another theory is that the kata was based on *Sasaki Kojiro's* sword techniques, because they were also said to resemble a swallow. The kata was practiced in the *Tomari-te* schools as early as 1683.

Characteristics: An advanced kata

Also known as: *Empi* or *Enpi* in *Shotokan,* meaning "flying swallow"

Used by: *Shotokan, Wado-ryu* and *Shorin-ryu*

GRADING KATA

Below are the lists of kata used for grading by the different styles of karate. They are in no particular order as the sub-styles will place different levels of importance on each.

Shotokan Kata

Bassai Dai
Bassai Sho
Chinte
Empi
Gangaku
Hangetsu
Heian Shodan
Heian Nidan
Heian Sandan
Heian Yondan
Heian Godan
Jitte
Ji'in
Jion
Kanku Dai
Kanku Sho
Meikyo
Nijushiho
Sochin
Tekki Shodan
Tekki Nidan
Tekki Sandan
Unsu

Shito-Ryu Kata

Aoyagi
Bassai Dai
Bassai Sho
Chatanyara Kushanku
Chintei
Chinto
Gojushi Ho
Heian Godan
Heian Nidan
Heian Sandan
Heian Shodan

Heian Yondan
Hiji Ate Go Ho
Itosu no Roahi Sandan
Itosu no Rohai Nidan
Itosu Rohai Shodan
Jiin
Jion
Jitte
Juni No Kata
Juroku
Koshokun Dai
Koshokun Sho
Kururunfa
Matsukaze
Matsumura Ha
Matsumura Ha Bassai
Myojo
Naifanchi Nidan
Naifanchi Sandan
Naifanchi Shodan
Nipaipo
Niseishi
Saifa
Sanchin
Sanseiru
Seienchin
Seipai
Seisan
Shiho Koshokun
Shinpa
Shinsei
Shinsei Ni
Shisochin
Suparinpei
Tomari no Bassai
Unsu
Wanshu

Goju-Ryu Kata

Gekisai Dai Ichi
Gekisai Dai Ni
Kururumfa
Saifa
Sanchin
Sanseiru
Seisan
Seiunchin
Sepai
Shisoshin
Suparimpei
Tensho

Wado-Ryu Kata

Chinto
Jion
Kusanku
Naihanchi
Neseishi
Passai
Pinan Godan
Pinan Nidan
Pinan Sandan
Pinan Shodan
Pinan Yondan
Rohai
Seisan
Suparimpei
Taikyoku Shodan
Unsu
Wanshu

Shorin-Ryu Kata

Chinto
Fyukyu No Kata
Gojushiho
Gorin No Kata
Kihon Ippon
Kihon Nihon
Kihon Sanbon
Kusanku Dai
Kusanku Sho
Nai Hanchi Nidan
Nai Hanchi Sandan
Nai Hanchi Shodan
Passai Dai
Passai Sho
Pinan Godan
Pinan Nidan
Pinan Sandan
Pinan Shodan
Pinan Yondan

*A **kobudo** kata being performed.*

CHAPTER 9

KATA COMPETITION RULES

ABOUT THE KATA COMPETITION RULES

The summary of *kata* rules listed below pertains to the World Karate Federation's (WKF) rules established in January 2009. As mentioned elsewhere in this book there are a number of karate associations to which a karateka or club may be affiliated, however, it is only WKF that is recognised by the International Olympic Committee. The rule book, so to speak, is divided into six articles with each article dealing with a specific topic. For example, Article 1 relates to the competition area, and Article 4 relates to The judging panel. These rules are updated and modified from time to time to increase the fairness of the event and reduce injuries.

ARTICLE 1 KATA COMPETITION AREA

For the proper performance of kata, a stable smooth surface is required. In most competitions the same matted area used in kumite are used for kata too.

ARTICLE 2 OFFICIAL DRESS

Competitors must wear the full karate outfit of *gi* pants and *gi* jacket together with the appropriate belt. Contestants who are incorrectly dressed are given one minute to don the correct clothing.

ARTICLE 3 ORGANIZATION OF KATA COMPETITIONS

Kata competitions may take the form of team and individual matches.

- Team matches consist of a competition between three person teams that are exclusively male or exclusively female.
- The individual kata match consists of individual performance in separate male and female divisions.
- Contestant elimination is based on the qualification system.
- The contestants must perform both compulsory (*shitei*) and free selection (*tokui*) kata during the competition. Only kata from WKF recognized schools of *Goju*, *Shito*, *Shoto*, and *Wado* systems will be accepted. See the schedule of the compulsory selection on page 107.

- No variation of the *shitei* kata is permitted, but contestants may choose from the list when performing *tokui* kata. Variations as taught by the contestant's school are permitted.

- The score table must be notified of the choice of kata prior to each round and contestants must perform a different kata in each round, including a qualifying round. However, contestants in the repechage may perform *shitei* or *tokui* kata. Once performed, a kata may not be repeated.

- In team kata competition bouts for medals, the teams must perform their chosen kata from the *tokui* list and, once complete, they must perform a demonstration of the meaning of the kata, the *bunkai*. The time allowed for the *bunkai* demonstration is five minutes and the official timekeeper will start the countdown clock as the team members perform the bow at the completion of the kata performance and will stop the clock at the final bow after the *bunkai* performance. Failing to complete the *bunkai* in this time will mean disqualification. It is important to note that the use of traditional weapons, ancillary equipment or additional apparel is not allowed.

A competition judge.

A junior kata practitioner.

*A **kobudo** kata being performed.*

ARTICLE 4 THE JUDGING PANEL

Each kata will be presided over by the chief judge who will sit in the center position facing the contestants and then another four judges will be seated at the corners of the competition area. Each judge will have a red and a blue flag or, if electronic scoreboards are being used, an input terminal.

ARTICLE 5 CRITERIA FOR DECISION

The judges pay attention to all the elements of karate namely:

- speed, power, balance, rhythm, and breathing (*kime*)
- meaning and understanding (*bunkai*)
- focus and concentration, and potential impact and form (*kihon*)
- traditional karate values and principles
- realism in fighting terms
- correct stances with proper tension, the legs and feet flat (*dachi*), and tension in the abdomen (*hara*)

Children performing katas.

Three karateka performing a kata in unison.

Three karateka beginning a kata in unison.

Aka and **ao** facing the chief kata judge.

Another key element in deciding who wins the bout is the level of difficulty of the kata performed. In other words, if two competitors both do their kata very well, the judges should vote for the person who performed the most difficult kata.

In team kata, synchronization without external cues (for example, music) is essential.

Disqualification occurs when a contestant:
- varies the *shitei* kata
- comes to a halt during the performance of a kata
- performs a kata different from that announced or as notified to the score table
- performs an ineligible kata or repeats a kata

ARTICLE 6 OPERATION OF MATCHES

Each bout starts with two contestants, one with a blue belt (*ao*) and one with a red belt (*aka*) answering their names in response to being summoned to the bout. They stand on the perimeter of the match area facing the chief kata judge and bow. *Ao* then steps back out of the match area. *Aka* then moves, as smartly as possible, to the start position of the chosen kata where a clear announcement of the name of the kata to be performed is made. *Aka* can then begin performing the kata. On completion of the kata, *aka* may bow and then leave the match area. Ao will begin and end the kata chosen by *ao* in the same manner. Both contestants return to the match area perimeter to await the decision by the judging panel.

A women's senior kata practitioner.

Contestants awaiting the judge's decision.

Ao *moving to the kata start position.*

The chief judge will call for a decision (*hantei*) and blow a two-tone blast on the whistle whereupon the judges will cast their votes immediately and without hesitation. The judges are required to hold their flags aloft for sufficient time for the flags to be counted and can only be lowered after the chief judge has given a short blast on his whistle. As there are an odd number of judges only one contestant can be voted the winner. The competitor who receives the majority of votes will be declared the winner by the caller/announcer and the competitors will bow to each other, then to the judging panel, and leave the match area.

The chief judge may call the other judges together if a kata does not conform to the rules or there is some other irregularity. The judges are then required to reach a verdict as to whether a contestant is to be disqualified. If a contestant is disqualified the chief judge will cross and uncross the flags.

Should a competitor fail to turn up when called or withdraws (*kiken*) the decision will be awarded automatically to the opponent without the need to perform the previously notified kata.

COMPETITION DOJO DIMENSIONS AND POSITIONING

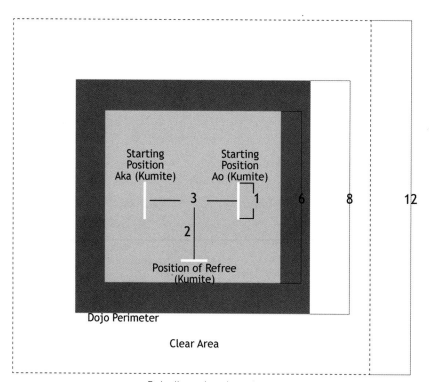

Dojo dimensions in meters.

WKF COMPETITION KATA

Below are the lists of compolsory and free selection kata used in WKF competitions. *Shorin-ryu* does not qualify for its own block of katas, their competitors generally perform katas from *Shito-ryu* block.

Shotokan

SHITEI (COMPULSORY) KATA

Jion

Kanku Dai

TOKUI (FREE SELECTION) KATA

1. *Bassai-Dai*
2. *Bassai-Sho*
3. *Kanku-Dai*
4. *Kanku-Sho*
5. *Tekki - Shodan*
6. *Tekki - Nidan*
7. *Tekki - Sandan*
8. *Hangetsu*
9. *Jitte*
10. *Enpi*
11. *Gankaku*
12. *Jion*
13. *Sochin*
14. *Nijushiho Sho*
15. *Goju Shiho-Dai*
16. *Goju Shiho-Sho*
17. *Chinte*
18. *Unsu*
19. *Meikyo*
20. *Wankan*
21. *Jiin*

Shito-Ryu

SHITEI (COMPULSORY) KATA

Bassai Dai

Seienchin

TOKUI (FREE SELECTION) KATA

1. *Jitte*
2. *Jion*
3. *Jiin*
4. *Matsukaze*
5. *Wanshu*
6. *Rohai*
7. *Passai Dai*
8. *Passai Sho*
9. *Tomari Bassai*
10. *Matsumura Bassai*
11. *Kusaku Dai*
12. *Kusanku Sho*
13. *Kusanku Shiho*
14. *Chinto*
15. *Chinte*
16. *Seienchin*
17. *Sochin*
18. *Niseishi*
19. *Gojushiho*
20. *Unshu*
21. *Seisan*
22. *Naihanchi Shoda*
23. *Naihanchi Nidan*
24. *Naihanchi Sandan*
25. *Aoyagi (Seiryu)*
26. *Jyuroku*
27. *Nipaipo*
28. *Sanchin*
29. *Tensho*
30. *Seipai*
31. *Sanseiru*
32. *Saifa*
33. *Shisochin*
34. *Kururunfa*
35. *Suparimpei*
36. *Hakucho*
37. *Pachu*
38. *Heiku*
39. *Paiku*
40. *Annan*
41. *Annanko*
42. *Papuren*
43. *Chatanyara Kusanku*

Goju-Ryu

SHITEI (COMPULSORY) KATA

Seipai

Saifa

TOKUI (FREE SELECTION) KATA

1. *Sanchin*
2. *Saifa*
3. *Seiyunchin*
4. *Shisochin*
5. *Sanseru*
6. *Seisan*
7. *Seipai*
8. *Kururunfa*
9. *Suparimpei*
10. *Tensho*

Wado-Ryu

SHITEI (COMPULSORY) KATA

Seishan

Chinto

TOKUI (FREE SELECTION) KATA

1. *Kushanku*
2. *Naihanchi*
3. *Seishan*
4. *Chinto*
5. *Passai*
6. *Niseishi*
7. *Rohai*
8. *Wanshu*
9. *Jion*
10. *Jitte*

Concentration and attitude is vital in **kumite.**

CHAPTER 10

KUMITE

KUMITE BASICS

Kumite is the use of karate techniques in sparring. A direct translation of kumite is "the coming together of hands." Without self-control kumite can result in very serious injury including broken bones, unconsciousness and even death, which means that it is essential that kumite only be practised with extreme care and restraint.

Experienced karateka will spar in a relaxed, accurate, and self-controlled manner with only light contact, and, although experienced karateka are capable of inflicting serious damage to an opponent, injuries seldom happen. When young or inexperienced karateka spar it is essential that the sensei maintains strict control to prevent injuries.

Kata training prepares karateka for kumite as all the techniques used in kata may be applied in kumite. Kumite in turn, enhances a karateka's kata speed, by improving their timing, self-control and fitness.

There are three types of kumite, namely light, medium or full contact. Light kumite involves "soft" contact or no contact with an opponent and is the only form of kumite that should be practiced by young and inexperienced karateka. Medium contact entails contact with an opponent that can cause pain but not disable the opponent and may be practiced by more senior karateka who are conditioned and capable of maintaining self-control. Full contact karate is reserved only for those karateka who are extremely fit and body conditioned and should only be performed under strict supervision by an experienced sensei. First aid facilities should also be available.

Karateka usually begin their kumite training with *ippon kumite* before progressing to *sanbon* and *gohon kumite*. Traditionally, both opponents face each other in a *yoi* position one arm's length apart before, on the sensei's command, adopting a stance appropriate to the techniques being practiced. The speed at which the techniques are applied increases as the karateka become more skilled and more familiar with the techniques being used. The techniques may be planned and then practiced to improve technical skill, but as karateka become more proficient these types of kumite may be practiced with no planning and the defender has to rely on speed and reflexes to execute an effective defense and counterattack.

In all forms of kumite, including competition kumite, opponents are required to show courtesy to each other and must bow to each other before and after fighting.

IPPON KUMITE

Ippon Kumite, also known as one step sparring, is the practice of a single attack and the defense thereof. Certain karate schools use *ippon kumite* as the first step to teaching *karateka* free style *kumite*. The fighting, for beginners, is very controlled with the attacker informing the defender exactly how they will attack before the fight begins.

On a more advanced level, the goal of the *ippon kumite* drills is to use the various techniques of karate to limit ones opponent to a single attack. One of the philosophies of karate, expressed through Sakugawa's *Dojo Kun*, is that a *karateka* should never be in a position were they are the first to strike. Another philosophy taught by many schools of karate is that an opponent can make only one attack and the consequence of that attack is a *karateka's* response, which is sufficiently powerful to ensure that the attacker is unable to attack a second time. Thus, *ippon kumite* teaches *karateka* to defend and counter an attack from an aggressor and ensure that they are unable to attack again.

The combinations of attack and defense are limitless. Perhaps the most simple would be for the attacker to strike with a *chudan-zuki* and the defender to block with an *uchi-uke* before striking with a *chudan zuki*. On a more advanced level, attacks could be in the form of an *ushiro mawashi geri* and the defense with a reverse sweep, which will then bring the attacker to the floor where the defender finishes off the attacker with a downward elbow strike to the throat.

*An example of **ippon kumite**—The karateka begin in **yoi** with the karateka on the right being the attacker and that on the left being the defender. The attacker begins with a lower stance (**zenkutsu-dachi**) and launches a punch. The defender blocks and launches a punch of his own. Both karateka return to **yoi**.*

SANBON AND GOHON KUMITE

Sanbon kumite is another form of controlled fighting. In this instance the attacker makes three attacks with the defender warding off all three before making an attack of his own that finishes off the attacker. A typical example would be the attacker starting with a *mae-geri-gedan*, followed by a *mawashi-geri-jodan* and then finishing with a *yoko-geri-chudan*. The defender blocks the *mae-geri* with a *gedan barai*, the *mawashi-geri* with a *soto-uke* and the *yoko-geri* with a *uchi-uke* before counter-attacking with an advanced application of an *uchi-uke* which leads to a take down.

With *gohon kumite* the attacker makes five attacks, all of which are defended before the defender attacks. Any combination of moves may be used before the defender counter attacks after the fifth attack.

*An example of **sanbon kumite** - The karateka begin in **yoi** with the karateka on the right being the attacker and that on the left being the defender. The attacker begins with a lower stance (**zenkutsu-dachi**) and launches his first attack, an upper (**jodan**) punch. The defender blocks and the attacker launches his next attack, a middle (**chudan**) punch, which the defender blocks too. The attacker launches the third and final attack, a front kick (**mae-geri**), which the defender blocks and then counter-attacks with a punch that hits the target. Both karateka return to **yoi**.*

YAKUSOKU KUMITE

Yakusoku kumite is a more advanced form of the above three types of *kumite* and some *yakusoko* sequences have over twenty-five moves. Whereas *ippon*, *sanbon*, and *gohon kumite* are usually linear, in other words they move along a single plane, backward and forward, *yakusoku kumite* is multidimensional. The *yakusoku kumite* of *Shorin-ryu*, of which there are seven commonly practiced forms, are identified by their number. So *yakusoku kumite* number one always follows the same sequence as does number two, and so on. As each style of karate have their own *yakusoku kumite* there are many hundreds of variations.

A direct translation of *yakosoku* means "promise to hit." Thus, opponents need to ensure that their distance, accuracy, speed and timing work together to ensure that there is contact with the opponent. Should the opponent fail to react effectively to an attack the opponent will be struck. *Yakosoku kumite* can also help with body conditioning as more experienced karateka can use greater strength, speed and force.

The step-by-step sequence of **Shorin–ryu Shorin-kan yokosoku three**.

JIYU KUMITE

Jiyu kumite is free sparring where no set techniques are used and opponents are free to use whatever moves they choose. Here karateka will improve on their reflexes and will find that they use kata techniques without thinking. The Japanese know this instinctual use of techniques as *mushin*.

Again, self-control should be maintained at all times and the sensei should maintain strict control of kumite classes.

Jiyu kumite.

CHAPTER 11

KUMITE COMPETITION RULES

ABOUT THE KUMITE COMPETITION RULES

Kumite involves a real opponent in a bout of free sparring. Kumite may involve various levels of contact from shadow to light to semi to full contact. The more contact, the fitter the participants must be. Full contact requires much body conditioning before participants can fight without being hurt by each strike or kick. As mentioned in Chapter 9, "Kata Competition Rules," this book focuses on WKF rules and here follows a summary of those rules.

ARTICLE 1: KUMITE COMPETITION AREA

To ensure that competitors are not injured when forced out of the competition area during a bout, advertisement boardings, walls, pillars or any other hard item, within one meter of the safety area's outer perimeter, are not permitted. The floor mats used in the competition area should be non-slip where they contact the floor proper, but also have a low coefficient of friction on the upper surface. It is the referee's responsibility to ensure that the mat modules do not move apart during the competition, since gaps cause injuries and constitute a hazard. The floor mats must be an approved WKF design. See the diagram on page 106 for the floor design.

ARTICLE 2: OFFICIAL DRESS

Contestants and their coaches must wear the official uniform as defined by WKF and the referee commission may disbar any official or competitor who does not comply.

Dress For Referees

Official dress of the referees:

- A single breasted navy blue blazer bearing two silver buttons
- A white shirt with short sleeves
- An official tie, worn without tiepin
- Plain light-gray trousers without turn-ups
- Plain dark blue or black socks and black slip-on shoes for use on the match area
- Female referees and judges may wear a hairclip

If the referee commission agrees the referees may remove their jackets.

Ippon (one full point)

Ippon (one full point)

Gyaku zuki is awarded one point

Dress For Contestants

Official dress of the contestants:

- A white karate gi without stripes or piping bearing the national emblem or flag on the left breast of the jacket and may not exceed an overall size of twelve centimeters by eight centimeters. The original manufacturer's labels may be displayed on the gi. Identification issued by the organizing committee will be worn on the back. One contestant must wear a red belt and the other a blue belt. The red and blue belts must be around five centimeters wide and of a length sufficient to allow fifteen centimeters free on each side of the knot. Competitors are advised to have a blue and a red belt of their own.

- The directing committee may authorize the display of special labels or trademarks of approved sponsors.

- The gi jacket, when tightened around the waist with the belt, must covers the hips, but must not reach more than three-quarters down the thigh.

- Female competitors may wear a plain white T-shirt beneath the karate jacket.

- The maximum length of the gi jacket sleeves must not reach further than the wrist and not be shorter than halfway down the forearm. Sleeves may not be rolled up.

- The trousers must be long enough to cover at least two-thirds of the shin and must not reach below the ankle bone. Trouser legs may not be rolled up.

- Hair must be clean and not obstruct smooth bout conduct. Headbands are not allowed. A referee may disbar a contestant from the bout for unclean or obstructive hair. Hair slides, headbands, metal hairgrips, ribbons, beads or any decorative items are prohibited. A discreet rubber band or ponytail retainer is permitted.

- Long fingernails are prohibited.

- No metallic or other objects may be worn that might injure an opponent. Metallic teeth braces must be approved by the referee and the official doctor. The contestant must accept full responsibility for any injury.

If a contestant comes into the area inappropriately dressed, he or she will not be immediately disqualified; instead they will be given one minute to remedy matters.

Compulsory Protective Equipment

All equipment must conform to WKF specifications.

- Mitts, one contestant wearing red and the other wearing blue. Contestants are advised to have one set of mitts in each color.

- Mouth guard that fits correctly.

- The female chest protector.

- Shin pads, one contestant wearing red and the other wearing blue.

- Foot protection, one contestant wearing red and the other wearing blue.

- Cadets must also wear a face mask and body protector.

- Groin guards are not mandatory but if worn must be of approved WKF type. Groin protectors using a removable plastic cup slipped into a jockstrap are not permitted and persons wearing them will be held at fault.

Forbidden equipment

The following equipment is forbidden for competitors:

- Glasses may not be worn but soft contact lenses can be worn at the contestant's own risk.

- Unauthorized apparel, clothing or equipment

All protective equipment must be WKF-approved and it is the duty of the arbitrator to ensure that, before each match or bout, the competitors are wearing the approved equipment. WKF-approved equipment cannot be refused. The use of bandages, padding, or supports because of injury must be approved by the referee on the advice of the official doctor.

Official Dress of Coaches

The official tracksuit of their national federation with a display of their official identification must be worn at all times during the tournament.

ARTICLE 3: ORGANIZATION OF KUMITE COMPETITIONS

A kata tournament may be divided into team matches and individual matches with individual matches being further divided into age and weight divisions. A "bout" describes the individual kumite competitions between opposing competitors. A "round" is the completion of all bouts in a particular stage in a competition leading to the eventual identification of finalists. In an elimination kumite competition, a round eliminates fifty percent of contestants within it. In this context, the round can apply equally to a stage in either primary elimination or qualification. In a matrix, or "round robin" competition, a round allows all contestants in a pool to fight once.

Nihon *(two points)*

Nihon *(two points)*

Chudan Mae-Geri *is awarded two points*

Chudan Mawashi-Geri *is awarded two points*

Sanbon *(three points)*

Sanbon *(three points)*

No contestant may be replaced by another in an individual title match and individual contestants or teams that do not present themselves when called will be disqualified from the category for which they have entered.

In team matches male teams comprise seven members with five competing in a round and female teams comprise four members with three competing in a round. There are no fixed reserves.

Before each match, a team representative must hand into the official table an official form giving the names and fighting order of the competing team members. The participants drawn from the full team of seven, or four members, and their fighting order, can be changed for each round provided the new fighting order is given to the official table first, but once given, it cannot then be changed until that round is completed. A team will be disqualified if its composition or fighting order is changed without written notification prior to the round.

As karateka and judges come from different parts of the world there is often a problem of name pronunciation and so identification tournament numbers should be allotted and used.

When lining up before a match, a team will present the actual fighters. The unused fighter(s) and the coach will not be included and shall sit in an area set aside for them. Male teams must present at least three competitors and female teams at least two competitors. A team with less than the required number of competitors will forfeit the match.

The fighting order form can be presented by the coach or a nominated contestant from the team. If the coach hands in the form, he must be clearly identifiable as such; otherwise, it may be rejected. The list must include the name of the country or club, the belt color allotted to the team for that match and the fighting order of the team members. Both the competitor's names and their tournament numbers must be included and the form signed by the coach, or a nominated person.

Coaches must present their accreditation together with that of their competitor or team to the official table. The coach must sit in the chair provided and must not interfere with the smooth running of the match by word or deed. If, through an error in charting, the wrong contestants compete, then regardless of the outcome, that bout/match is declared null and void. To reduce such errors the winner of each bout/match must confirm victory with the control table before leaving the area.

ARTICLE 4: THE REFEREE PANEL

The refereeing panel for each match consists of one referee *(shushin)*, three judges *(fukushin)*, and one arbitrator *(kansa)*. The referee and judges may not be of the same nationality as either of the contestants. The facilitation of each match is done by several timekeepers, caller announcers, record keepers, and score supervisors.

At the start of a kumite match, the referee stands on the outside edge of the competition area and on his left stand judges number one and two and on his right stands the arbitrator and judge number three. After the formal exchange of bows by contestants and the referee panel, the referee takes a step back, the judges and arbitrator turn inward, and all bow together. All then take up their positions. When changing the entire refereeing panel, the departing officials take up position as at the start of the bout or match, bow to each other, and then leave the area together. When individual judges change, the incoming judge goes to the outgoing judge, they bow together and change positions.

Jodan Mawashi-Geri *is awarded three points*

ARTICLE 5: DURATION OF BOUTS

Here are the rules pertaining to the duration of a bout:

- Senior male kumite (both teams and individuals) is three minutes and four minutes in the individual bouts for medals.

- Senior female bouts will be two minutes and three minutes in the individual bouts for medals.

- Cadet and junior bouts will be two minutes.

- The timing of a bout begins when the referee gives the signal to start, and stops each time the referee calls *"yame."*

- The timekeeper shall give signals by a clearly audible gong or buzzer which will indicate "ten seconds to go" and "time up." The "time up" signal marks the end of the bout.

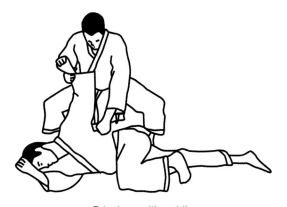

*Takedown with a strike
is awarded three points*

ARTICLE 6: SCORING

Judges and referees will look at two aspects to decide on whether a score is awarded or not:

- Score will only be awarded for strikes, punches or kicks to the following seven areas: head, face, neck, abdomen, chest, back, and side.

- A score is awarded when a technique is performed to the following criteria to a scoring area: good form, sporting attitude, vigorous application, awareness (termed *zanshin)*, good timing, and correct distance.

Jogai *(outside the contest area)*

Jogai *(outside the contest area)*

Excessive force

Tzuzukete Hajime *(begin or resume fighting)*

Scoring Criteria

Description of good scoring criteria:

- Good form is the probable effectiveness of the punch, kick or strike within the framework of traditional karate concepts.

- Sporting attitude refers to a non-malicious attitude during delivery of the scoring technique.

- Vigorous application is the power and speed of the technique and the palpable will for it to succeed.

- Awareness *(zanshin)* is the continued commitment in which the contestant maintains total concentration, observation, and awareness of the opponent's potentiality to counter-attack.

- Good timing means delivering a technique when it will have the greatest potential effect.

- Correct distance is the delivering of a technique at the precise distance where it will have the greatest potential effect. If the technique is delivered on an opponent who is rapidly moving away the potential effect of that blow is reduced. Distancing also relates to the point at which the completed technique comes to rest on or near the target. A punch or kick that comes somewhere between skin touch and five centimetres from the face, head, or neck may be said to have the correct distance. However, *jodan* techniques, which come within a reasonable distance of the target and which the opponent makes no attempt to block or avoid will be scored, provided the technique meets the other criteria. In cadet and junior competition no contact to the head, face, or neck, (or the face mask) is allowed other than a very light touch (previously known as a "skin touch") for *jodan* kicks and the scoring distance is increased up to ten centimeters.

Scoring Values

The value of scores are as follows:

Sanbon—Three points are awarded for:

- *Jodan* kicks to the face, head and neck area.

- Any scoring technique that is delivered on an opponent who has been thrown, has fallen of their own accord, or is otherwise off their feet.

Nihon—Two points are awarded for:

- *Chudan* kicks to the abdomen, chest, back and side.

Ippon—One point is awarded for:

- Any punch (*tsuki*) delivered to any of the seven scoring areas.

- Any strike (*uchi*) delivered to any of the seven scoring areas.

No score is awarded when:

- A technique, even if effective, is delivered after an order to suspend or stop the bout has been issued and may result in a penalty being imposed on the offender.

- No technique, even if technically correct, will be scored if it is delivered when the two contestants are outside the competition area. However, if one of the contestants delivers an effective technique while still inside the competition area and before the referee calls *"yame,"* the technique will be scored.

- Simultaneous, effective scoring techniques delivered by both contestants, the one on the other (known as *aiuchi)* shall not score. This is very rare as all the criterea listed in this article have to occur at the same time from each opponent.

Yame *(stop fighting)*

Scoring Throws and Sweeps

The following rules apply to throws and sweeps when scoring *sanbon*:

- Throws where the opponent is grabbed below the waist, thrown without being held onto or thrown dangerously or where the pivot point is above hip level, are prohibited and will incur a warning or penalty.

- Exceptions are conventional karate leg sweeping techniques, which do not require the opponent to be held while executing the sweep such as *de ashi-barai, ko uchi gari, kani waza,* and the like.

- After a throw has been executed the referee will allow the contestant two seconds in which to attempt a scoring technique.

Scoring Throws and Sweeps

Other considerations when scoring:

- An effective technique delivered at the same time that the end of the bout is signalled, is considered valid.

- Techniques that land below the belt but above the pubic bone do score.

- The neck and throat are target areas but no contact to the throat is permitted, although a score may be awarded for a properly controlled technique, which does not touch.

- A technique that lands upon the shoulder blades may score. The non-scoring part of the shoulder is the junction of the upper bone of the arm with the shoulder blades and collarbones.

- The time-up bell signals the end of scoring possibilities in that bout, even though the referee may inadvertently not halt the bout immediately.

No Kachi Aka *(winner is **aka**)*

Hikiwake *(tie match)*

Category 1 offense

Category 2 offense

Keikoku *(ippon penalty)*

Penalties

The time-up bell does not, however, mean that penalties cannot be imposed. Penalties can be imposed by the refereeing panel up to the point when the contestants leave that area after the bout's conclusion. Penalties can be imposed after that, but then only by the referee commission or the disciplinary and legal commission.

ARTICLE 7: CRITERIA FOR A DECISION

The result of a bout is determined by:

- A contestant obtaining a clear lead of eight points.
- Or, at time-up, having the highest number of points.
- Or, obtaining a decision by *hantei*.
- Or, by a *hansoku*, *shikkaku*, or *kiken* imposed against a contestant.

Tie Bouts (*Hikiwake*)

In the case of a tie, termed *hikiwake*, in an individual bout an extra deciding bout not exceeding one minute will be fought termed *sai shiai*. A *sai shiai* is a new bout starting, on zero score for each competitor, at the end of which a winner will be declared. If at the end of this bout the competitors still have an equal score a decision will be made by a final vote, termed *hantei*, of the referee and three judges. A decision in favor of one or the other competitor is obligatory and is taken on the basis of the following criteria;

- The attitude, fighting spirit, and strength demonstrated by the contestants.
- The superiority of tactics and techniques displayed.
- Which of the contestants has initiated the majority of the action.

In team competitions the winning team is:

- The one with the most bout victories.
- Or, should the two teams have the same number of bout victories then the winning team will be the one with the most points, taking both winning and losing bouts into account. The maximum point's difference or lead recorded in any bout will be eight.
- If the two teams have the same number of bout victories and points, then a deciding bout will be held.
- In the event of a continuing tie, there will be an extra bout (*sai shiai*) not exceeding one minute.

- In the event that there is no score, or scores are equal, the decision will be made by vote of the referee and three judges (*hantei*).

- When a team has won sufficient bout victories or scored sufficient points as to be the established winner then the match is declared over and no further bouts will take place.

Procedure for *hantei* decisions:

- The referee will move to the match area perimeter and call "*hantei*," followed by a two-tone blast of the whistle.

- The judges will indicate their opinions by means of their flags and the referee will at the same time indicate his own vote by raising his arm on the side of the preferred contestant.

- The referee will give a short blast on his whistle, return to his original position and announce the majority decision.

- In the event of a tied vote, the referee will resolve the tie by use of his casting vote. On returning to his original position, the referee will place one arm across his chest and raise his bent arm on the side of the preferred choice to show he is using his casting vote. He will then indicate the winner in the normal way.

Hansoku chui (*nihon penalty*)

ARTICLE 8: PROHIBITED BEHAVIOR

Competition karate is a sport and thus the most dangerous techniques are banned and all techniques must be controlled. No matter how fit or strong a competitor is, the head, face, neck, groin and joints are particularly susceptible to injury and any technique that results in injury may be penalized unless caused by the recipient.

Karateka are also trained to hurt and thus all techniques must be applied with control and good form to prevent injuries. If any technique is misused a warning or penalty will be imposed. Cadets and junior competitors have less skill and body conditioning, thus particular care must be exercised to prevent injuries. There are two categories of prohibited behavior:

Category 1—Prohibited Attacking Behavior

The following are prohibited attacking behaviors:

- Techniques that make excessive contact, having regard to the scoring area attacked, and techniques that make contact with the throat.

- Attacks to the arms or legs, groin, joints, or instep.

- Attacks to the face with open hand techniques.

- Dangerous or forbidden throwing techniques.

Hansoku (*disqualification*)

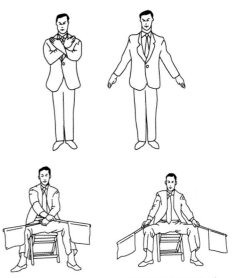

Torimasen (*no score, unacceptable scoring*)

Aiuchi *(simultaneous scoring)*

Category 2—Prohibited Non-Attacking Behavior

The following are prohibited non-attacking behaviors:

- Feigning, or exaggerating injury.

- Repeated exits from the competition area, termed *jogai*.

- Self-endangerment by indulging in behavior that exposes the contestant to injury by the opponent, or failing to take adequate measures for self-protection, termed *mubobi*.

- Avoiding combat as a means of preventing the opponent having the opportunity to score.

- Clinching, wrestling, pushing, seizing or standing chest to chest, without attempting a throw or other technique.

- Techniques, which by their nature, cannot be controlled for the safety of the opponent and dangerous and uncontrolled attacks.

- Simulated attacks with the head, knees or elbows.

- Talking to, or goading the opponent,

- Failing to obey the orders of the referee, discourteous behavior towards the refereeing officials, or other breaches of etiquette.

Contact to the Face, Head and Neck

For senior competitors a non-injurious, light touch to the face, head, and neck is allowed—but not to the throat. Strong contact that does not diminish the competitor's chances of winning will result in a warning, termed *chukoku*. If it happens a second time in the same bout the offender will be penalized by *keikoku* and one point (*ippon*) will be given to the opponent. Should it happen a third time in the same bout the offender will be given *hansoku chui* and two points (*nihon*) will be given to the injured competitor. A forth offence will result in disqualification by *hansoku*. The same rules apply to cadet and junior competitors except that any touch or contact to the head, neck or face, including the face mask, no matter how light, will be penalized. *Jodan* kicks may make the lightest touch and still score.

Faking Injury

The referee will constantly observe the injured contestant as a short delay in giving a judgement allows injury symptoms such as a nosebleed to develop. In addition, it is possible that the injured party may aggravate a slight injury for tactical advantage.

Examples being blowing violently through an injured nose, or rubbing the face roughly. Pre-existing injury can produce symptoms out of all proportion to the degree of contact used and referees must take this into account when considering penalties for seemingly excessive contact. The match area controller must examine the medical cards and ensure that the contestants are fit to fight before a bout. The referee must be informed if a contestant has been treated for injury. As the throat is a particularly vulnerable area and even the slightest contact will be warned or penalized, unless it is the recipient's own fault.

Overreaction to Injuries

Over reaction by an injured party will result in the injured party being penalized with a *shikkaku* (see definition on page 127). Exaggerating the effect of an actual injury in the first instance of exaggeration will receive a minimum penalty of *keikoku* and *ippon* to the opponent. A more serious exaggeration such as staggering around, falling on the floor, standing up and falling down again, and so on may receive *hansoku chui* or *hansoku* directly depending on the severity of the offense. Competitors who receive *shikkaku* for feigning injury will be taken from the competition area and put directly into the hands of the WKF medical commission, who will carry out an immediate examination of the competitor. The medical commission will submit its report before the end of the championship, for the consideration of the referee commission. Competitors who feign injury will be subject to the strongest penalties, up to and including suspension for life for repeated offences.

Forbidden Throws

The following are forbidden throws:

- Over the shoulder throws.
- Sacrifice throws.
- Grabbing the opponent below the waist and lifting and throwing.
- Reaching down to pull the legs from under an opponent.

If a contestant is injured as a result of a throwing technique, the referee panel will decide whether a penalty is called for.

Stepping Outside the Match Area

Jogai is the term used to describe being outside a match area and refers to any part of the body. An exception is when the contestant is physically pushed or thrown from the area by the opponent. Note the following:

- A contestant who delivers a scoring technique then exits the area before the referee calls *"yame"* will be given the value of the score and *jogai* will not be imposed. If the contestant's attempt to score is unsuccessful the exit will be recorded as a *jogai*.

- If a competitor exits just after the opponent scores with a successful attack, then *"yame"* will occur immediately on the score and the competitor's exit will not be recorded. If the competitor exits, or has exited as the opponent's score is made with the scorer remaining within the area, then the score will be awarded and the *jogai* penalty will be imposed.

Avoiding Combat

Contestants may be penalized for avoiding combat. A contestant who seeks to avoid scoring or preventing an opponent from scoring by avoiding combat will be warned or penalized in the following instances:

- If the offence occurs with ten seconds or more of the bout time remaining the referee will warn the offender.
- If there has been a previous category 2 offence or offenses, this will result in a penalty being imposed.
- If there are less than ten seconds to go, the referee will penalize the offender with *keikoku* regardless of whether there has been a previous category 2 *chukoku* or not and award an *ippon* to the opponent.
- f there has been a previous category 2 *keikoku* the referee will penalize the offender with *hansoku chui* and award *nihon* to the opponent.
- If there has been a previous category 2 *hansoku chui* the referee will penalize the offender with *hansoku* and award the bout to the opponent.

However, the referee must ensure that the contestant's behavior is not a defensive measure due to the opponent acting in a reckless or dangerous manner, in which case the attacker should be warned or penalized.

Personal Endangerment

Personal endangerment is known as *mubobi* and includes but is not limited to:

- A contestant who launches a committed attack without regard for personal safety. Such open attacks constitute an act of *mubobi* and cannot score.

- A tactical theatrical move where a fighter turns away immediately in a mock display of dominance to demonstrate a scored point. In doing so they drop their guard. This is also a clear act of *mubobi* and should the offender receive an excessive contact and/or sustain an injury the referee will issue a category 2 warning or penalty and decline to give a penalty to the opponent.

Discourtesy

Any discourteous behavior from a member of an official delegation can earn the disqualification of a competitor, the entire team or delegation from the tournament.

ARTICLE 9: WARNING AND PENALTIES

When awarding warnings and penalties it must be noted that:

- Warnings and penalties may be awarded for both category 1 and category 2 prohibited behavior but these warnings and penalties do not cross-accumulate.

- Once a warning or penalty is given, repeats of that category of infraction must be accompanied by an increase in severity of penalty imposed. It is not, for example, possible to give a warning or penalty for excessive contact then give another warning for a second instance of excessive contact.

Chukoku: Is a warning and may be imposed for minor infractions or the first instance of a minor infraction and were the contestant's potential for winning is not diminished (in the opinion of the referee panel) by the opponent's foul.

Keikoku: Is a penalty in which one point (*ippon*), is added to the opponent's score. *Keikoku* is imposed for minor infractions for which a warning has previously been given in that bout. *Keikoku* may be also be imposed without first giving a warning. *Keikoku* is normally imposed directly where the contestant's potential for winning is slightly diminished (in the opinion of the referee panel) by the opponent's foul.

Hansoku-chui: Is a penalty in which two points (*Nihon*), is added to the opponent's score. *Hansoku-chui* is usually imposed for infractions for which a *keikoku* has previously been given in that bout although it may be imposed directly where the contestant's potential for winning has been seriously reduced (in the opinion of the referee panel) by the opponent's foul.

Hansoku: Is imposed following a very serious infraction as when the contestant's potential for winning has been reduced virtually to zero (in the opinion of the referee panel) by the opponent's foul or it may be awarded when a *hansoku-chui* has already been given. It results in the disqualification of the contestant. In team matches the fouled competitor's score will be set at eight points and the offender's score will be zeroed. Any competitor who receives *Hansoku* for causing injury, and who has, in the opinion of the referee panel and match area controller, acted recklessly or dangerously or who is considered not to have the requisite control skills necessary for WKF competition, will be reported to the referee commission. The referee commission will decide if that competitor shall be suspended from the rest of that competition and/or subsequent competitions.

Shikkaku: This is a disqualification from the actual tournament, competition, or match. In order to define the limit of *shikkaku*, the referee commission must be consulted. *Shikkaku* may be invoked when a contestant fails to obey the orders of the Referee, acts maliciously, or commits an act which harms the prestige and honor of *karate-do*, or when other actions are considered to violate the rules and spirit of the tournament. In team matches the fouled competitor's score will be set at eight points and the offender's score will be zeroed. A *shikkaku* can be directly imposed, without warnings of any kind. A contestant may be invoked with a *shikkaku* if the coach or non-combatant members of the contestant's delegation behave in such a way as to harm the prestige and honor of *karate-do*. If the referee believes that a contestant has acted maliciously, regardless of whether or not actual physical injury has been caused, *shikkaku* and not *hansoku*, is the correct penalty. A public announcement of *shikkaku* must be made.

ARTICLE 10: INJURIES AND ACCIDENTS IN COMPETITION

Forfeiture Decisions

Kiken or forfeiture is the decision given when:

- A contestant or contestants fail to present themselves when called.
- A contestant or contestants are unable to continue.
- A contestant or contestants abandon the bout (grounds for abandonment may include injury not ascribable to the opponent's actions).
- A contestant or contestants are withdrawn on the order of the referee.

Forfeiture decisions due to injuries unconnected with excessive force by one participant:

- If two contestants injure each other or are suffering from the effects of previously incurred injury, and are declared by the tournament doctor to be unable to continue, the bout is awarded to the contestant who has amassed the most points.
- In Individual matches if the points score is equal, then a vote (*hantei*) will decide the outcome of the bout.
- In Team matches the Referee will announce a tie (*hikiwake*). Should the situation occur in a deciding team match *sai shiai* then a vote (*hantei*) will determine the outcome. An injured contestant who has been declared unfit to fight by the tournament doctor cannot fight again in that competition.

Consequences of Disqualification

Consequences of disqualification for the undisqualified opponent:

- An injured contestant who wins a bout through disqualification due to injury is not allowed to fight again in the competition without permission from the doctor. If he is injured, he may win a second bout by disqualification but is immediately withdrawn from further *kumite* competition in that tournament.
- A contestant may win through disqualification of the opponent for accumulated minor category 1 infractions. Perhaps the winner has sustained no significant injury. A second win on the same grounds must lead to withdrawal, even though the contestant may be physically able to continue.

Injuries

Dealing with injuries:

- When a contestant is injured, the referee shall at once halt the bout and call the doctor. The doctor is authorized to diagnose, treat injury and make safety recommendations pertaining to the injured party only.

- A competitor who is injured during a bout in progress and requires medical treatment will be allowed three minutes in which to receive it. If treatment is not completed within the time allowed, the referee will decide if the competitor shall be declared unfit to fight, or whether an extension of treatment time shall be given. When the doctor declares the contestant unfit, the appropriate entry must be made on the contestant's monitoring card. The extent of unfitness must be made clear to other refereeing panels.

- Any competitor who falls, is thrown, or knocked down, and does not fully regain his or her feet within ten seconds, is considered unfit to continue fighting and will be automatically withdrawn from all *kumite* events in that tournament. In the event that a competitor falls, is thrown, or knocked down and does not regain his or her feet immediately, the referee will signal to the timekeeper to start the ten second count-down by a blast on his whistle, at the same time calling the doctor. The timekeeper will stop the clock when the referee raises his arm. In all cases where the ten second clock has been started the doctor will be asked to examine the contestant. When applying the "ten second rule" the time will be kept by a timekeeper appointed for this specific purpose. A warning will be sounded at seven seconds followed by the final bell at ten seconds. The time keeper may only stop the clock when when the competitor stands fully upright and the referee raises his arm.

ARTICLE 11: OFFICIAL PROTEST

Complaints

Procedure for lodging a complaint:

- Protests can only be submitted to a member of the appeals jury and never to the refereeing panel. The sole exception is when the protest concerns an administrative malfunction. The match area controller should be notified immediately that the administrative malfunction is detected, and will then notify the referee. The protest must be accompanied by a protest fee. Ensuing matches or bouts will not be delayed, even if an official protest is being prepared.

- If a refereeing procedure appears to contravene the rules, the president of the federation or the official representative is the only one allowed to make a protest and this protest can only be done in writing and must be submitted immediately after the disputed bout is finished. The protest must give the names of the contestants, the referee panel officiating, and the precise details of what is being protested. The burden of proving the validity of the protest lies with the complainant. The protest must be signed by the official representative of the team or contestant(s).

- The appeals jury will, in due course, review the circumstances leading to the protested decision. Having considered all the facts available, they will produce a report, and shall be empowered to take such action as may be called for.

Appeals Panels

Composition of the appeals panel:

- The appeals jury is comprised of three senior referee representatives appointed by the referee commission (RC).

- No two members may be appointed from the same national federation.

- The RC should also appoint three additional members with designated numbering from one to three that will automatically replace any of the originally appointed appeals jury members in a conflict of interest situation.

Appeals Evaluation Process

It is the responsibility of the party receiving the protest to convene the appeals jury and deposit the protest sum with the treasurer. Once convened, the appeals jury will immediately make such inquiries and investigations, as they deem necessary to substantiate the merit of the protest. The jury may also study videos and question officials, in an effort to objectively examine the protest's validity. Each of the three members is obliged to give his/her verdict as to the validity of the protest. Abstentions are not acceptable.

Declined Protests

If a protest is found invalid, the appeals jury will appoint one of its members to verbally notify the protester that the protest has been declined, mark the original document with the word "DECLINED," and have it signed by each of the members of the appeals jury, before depositing the protest with the treasurer, who in turn will forward it to the secretary general. The deposit is forfeited to WKF.

Accepted Protests

If a protest is accepted, the appeals jury will liaise with the organizing commission (OC) and referee commission to take such measures as can be practically carried out to remedy the situation including the possibilities of:

- Reversing previous judgments that contravene the rules.
- Voiding results of the affected matches in the pool from the point previous to the incident.
- Redoing such matches that have been affected by the incident.
- Issuing a recommendation to the RC that involved referees are evaluated for correction or sanction.

The responsibility rests with the appeals jury to exercise restraint and sound judgment in taking actions that will disturb the program of the event in any significant manner. Reversing the process of the eliminations is a last option to secure a fair outcome. The appeals jury will appoint one of its members who will verbally notify the protester that the protest has been accepted, mark the original document with the word "ACCEPTED," and have it signed by each of the members of the appeals jury, before depositing the protest with the treasurer, who will return the deposited amount to the protester, and in turn forward the protest document to the secretary general. In addition, all such measures will be taken to avoid a recurrence in future competitions.

Incident Report

Subsequent to handling the incident in the above prescribed manner, the jury panel will reconvene and elaborate a simple protest incident report, describing their findings and state their reason(s) for accepting or rejecting the protest. The report should be signed by all three members of the appeals jury and submitted to the secretary general.

Power and Constraints

The decision of the appeals jury is final, and can only be overruled by a decision of the executive committee. The appeals jury may not impose sanctions or penalties. Their function is to pass judgment on the merit of the protest and instigate required actions from the RC and OC to take remedial action to rectify any refereeing procedure found to contravene the rules.

ARTICLE 12: POWERS AND DUTIES

The Referee Commission's Powers and Duties

The referee commission's powers and duties shall be as follows:

- To ensure the correct preparation for each given tournament in consultation with the organizing commission, with regard to competition area arrangement, the provision and deployment of all equipment and necessary facilities, match operation and supervision, safety precautions, etc.

- To appoint and deploy the match area controllers (chief referees) to their respective areas and to act upon and take such action as may be required by the reports of the match area controllers.

- To supervise and co-ordinate the overall performance of the refereeing officials.

- To nominate substitute officials where such are required.

- To pass the final judgement on matters of a technical nature that may arise during a given match and for which there are no stipulations in the rules.

The Match Area Controller's Powers and Duties

The match area controller's powers and duties shall be as follows:

- To delegate, appoint, and supervise the referees and judges, for all matches in areas under their control.

- To oversee the performance of the referees and judges in their areas, and to ensure that the officials appointed are capable of the tasks allotted them.

- To order the referee to halt the match when the arbitrator signals a contravention of the rules of competition.

- To prepare a daily, written report, on the performance of each official under their supervision, together with their recommendations, if any, to the referee commission.

The Referee's Powers

The referee's powers shall be as follows:

- The referee (*shushin*) shall have the power to conduct matches including announcing the start, the suspension, and the end of the match.

- To award points.

- To explain to the match area controller, referee commission, or appeals jury, if necessary, the basis for giving a judgement.

- To impose penalties and to issue warnings, before, during, or after a bout.

- To obtain and act upon the opinion(s) of the judges.

- To announce and start an extra bout (*sai shiai*).

- To conduct voting of the referee panel (*hantei*) and announce the result.

- To resolve ties.

- To announce the winner.

- The authority of the referee is not confined solely to the competition area but also to all of its immediate perimeter.

- The referee shall give all commands and make all announcements.

The Judge's Powers

The judge's (*fukushin*) powers shall be as follows:

- To assist the referee by flag signals.

- To exercise a right to vote on a decision to be taken.

The judges shall carefully observe the actions of the contestants and signal to the referee an opinion in the following cases:

- When a score is observed.

- When a contestant has committed a prohibited act and/or techniques.

- When an injury, illness or inability of a contestant to continue is noticed.

- When both or either of the contestants have moved out of the competition area (*jogai*).

- In other cases when it is deemed necessary to call the attention of the referee.

The arbitrator (*kansa*) will assist the match area controller by overseeing the match or bout in progress. The role of the arbitrator is to ensure that the match or bout is conducted in accordance within the rules of competition. He is not there as an additional judge. He has no vote, nor has he any authority in matters of judgement. His sole responsibility is in matters of procedure. Should decisions of the referee and/or judges not be in accordance with the rules of competition, the arbitrator will immediately raise the red flag and blow his whistle. The match area controller will instruct the referee to halt the match or bout and correct the irregularity. Records kept of the match shall become official records subject to the approval of the arbitrator. Before the start of each match or bout the arbitrator will ensure that the contestants are wearing approved equipment. Should the referee fail to stop the bout when three judges give the same signal the arbitrator will raise the red flag and blow his whistle. When two judges give the same signal, or indicate a score for the same competitor, the referee will consider their opinions but may decline to stop the bout if he believes them to be mistaken. However, when the bout is halted, the majority decision will prevail.

The score supervisor will keep a separate record of the scores awarded by the referee and at the same time oversee the actions of the appointed timekeepers and scorekeepers. In the event that the referee does not hear the time-up bell, the score-supervisor will blow his whistle.

The Referee's Responsibilities

The referee's responsibilities when scoring:

- When the referee decides to halt the bout he will call "*yame*" at the same time using the required hand signal. The judges will lower their flags and await the referee's opinion. When the referee returns to his starting line, he will convey his reason(s) for stopping the bout by using the appropriate signal(s). The judges will then signal their opinions and the referee will render the majority decision.

- In the event of a two/two decision the referee will indicate with the appropriate signal why the other contestant's score is not considered to be valid and then award the score to the opponent.

- When three judges each have different opinions, the referee may give a decision, which is supported by one of the judges.

- In the event that two judges fail to signal and the other is in disagreement with the referee, then the referee will decide what action to take.

- At *hantei* the referee and judges each have one vote. In the event of a tied *sai shiai* the referee will have a casting vote.

The Judge's Responsibilities

The judge's responsibilities when scoring:

The judges must only score what they actually see. If they are not sure that a technique actually reached a scoring area, they should not signal.

ARTICLE 13: STARTING, SUSPENDING AND ENDING OF MATCHES

Starting

When starting a match:

- The referee and judges shall take up their prescribed positions.

- The referee first calls the contestants to their starting lines. If a contestant enters the area prematurely, they must be motioned off. The contestants must bow properly to each other (a quick nod is both discourteous and insufficient). The referee can call for a bow where none is volunteered by motioning.

- The referee will announce "*shobu hajime*!" and the bout will commence.

Suspending

When suspending a match:

- The referee will stop the bout by announcing "*yame.*" If necessary, the referee will order the contestants to take up their original positions (*moto noichi*).

- The referee returns to his position and indicates his opinion; the judges then indicate their opinion by means of a signal. In the case of a score to be awarded the referee identifies the contestant (*aka* or *ao*), the area attacked (*chudan* or *jodan*), the scoring technique (*tsuki*, *uchi*, or *keri*), and then awards the relevant score using the prescribed gesture.

- When faced with the following situations, the referee will call "*yame*!" and halt the bout temporarily:
  - When either or both contestants are out of the match area.
  - When the referee orders the contestant to adjust the karate gi or protective equipment.
  - When a contestant has contravened the rules.
  - When the referee considers that one or both of the contestants cannot continue with the bout owing to injuries, illness, or other causes. Heeding the tournament doctor's opinion, the referee will decide whether the bout should be continued.
  - When a contestant seizes the opponent and does not perform an immediate technique, or throw within two seconds.
  - When one or both contestants fall or are thrown and no effective techniques are made within two seconds.
  - When both competitors seize or clinch with each other without attempting a throw or technique within two seconds.
  - When both competitors stand chest to chest without attempting a throw or other technique within two seconds.
  - When both contestants are off their feet following a fall or attempted throw and begin to wrestle.
  - When a score is observed.
  - When three judges give the same signal, or indicate a score for the same competitor.
  - When requested to do so by the match area controller.

Restarting

The Referee then restarts the bout by calling "*tsuzukete hajime.*"

When restarting the bout, the referee should check that both contestants are on their lines and properly composed. Contestants jumping up and down or otherwise fidgeting must be stilled before combat can recommence. The referee must restart the bout with the minimum of delay.

Ending

When a contestant has established a clear lead of eight points during a bout, the referee shall call "*yame*" and order the contestants back to their starting lines as he returns to his. The winner is then declared and indicated by the referee raising a hand on the side of the winner and declaring "*ao* (or) *aka no kachi.*" The bout is ended at this point.

When time is up, the contestant who has the most points is declared the winner, indicated by the referee raising a hand on the side of the winner, and declaring "*ao* (or) *aka no kachi.*" The bout is ended at this point. Contestants will bow to each other at the end of each bout.

Restarting from a Draw

When time is up and scores are equal, or no scores have been awarded, the referee shall call "*yame*" and return to his position. He will announce a tie (*hikiwaki*) and start the *sai shiai* if applicable.

At *hantei* the referee and judges each have one vote. In the event of a tied vote at the end of an inconclusive *sai shiai* the referee will have a casting vote that will be used to break the tie.

ARTICLE 14: MODIFICATIONS

Only the WKF sports commission, with the approval of the WKF executive committee, can alter or modify the rules.

Effective use of the ulna.

CHAPTER 12

BODY HARD POINTS

The human body has a number of points where solid, well-supported bone lies close to the surface, and in some instances, has very little in the way of nerves. These hard points are ideal for striking, blocking, or kicking an opponent as they will do much damage. These points include:

- Top of the skull
- Ulna
- Radius
- Pisiform carpal
- Proximal phalanges
- Tibia

TOP OF THE SKULL (CRANIUM)

This is perhaps the strongest bone in the body as it is designed to protect one of the body's most vital organs, the brain. When using the skull ensure that only the top half of the skull is used, whether it is the side, forehead or back of the head. Never use any point from the eyebrows and ears and below, preferably using only points one centimeter or higher than the ears and eyebrows. There are two disadvantages to using the skull, the first is that if the skin is broken, the skull bleeds profusely and if the blood runs into the eyes it can limit vision. Second, hard, solid strikes to the skull can cause concussion. When using the skull ensure that you bring it into contact with softer parts of the opponent's body such as the eyebrows or nose.

Effective use of the cranium.

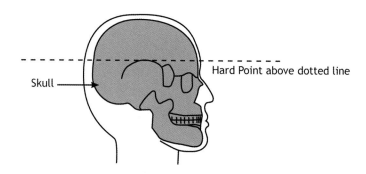

Skull ——

Hard Point above dotted line

*The hard point of the skull lies above the eyebrows
and ears only. Never use the lower part of the
skull for striking purposes.*

ULNA

The ulna, one of two bones found in the forearm, is a fantastic weapon, and has two hard points. The first is the area two finger-widths down from the elbow, and extending three finger-widths towards the hand. This area is very hard, the bone being close to the surface, and has few nerves. Elbow strikes make use of this point of contact. This section is also very good for blocking kicks, especially *chudan* and *jodan mawashi-geris*. A solid block to the opponent's foot will ensure that he does not walk for some time.

The second hard point on the ulna is the area from the wrist to one hand-width down the forearm towards the elbow. This area is not as solid as the opposite end of the ulna, but is the point of contact when performing *soto-uke, gedan-uke* and *age-uke*.

The impact points on the ulna are narrow and surrounded by areas that are very vulnerable, including the mass of veins near the wrist.

Effective use of the ulna in a **hiji-zuki**.

Effective use of the ulna through a **soto-uke**.

RADIUS:

The area three finger-widths up the radius from the wrist is not a particularly hard area as it has a number of small nerve endings and relatively thick flesh. One of the reasons why *kung-fu* artists use the wooden dummy is to toughen this area. *Uchi-uke* impacts on this area.

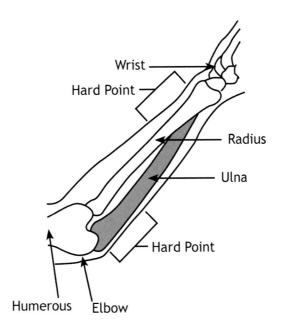

Diagram of the ulna and radius.

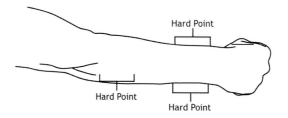

The forearm's hardpoints.

PISIFORM CARPAL

This small bone is well embedded into the hand and is of great use against an opponent's pressure points. This hard point is used in the *shotei* strike. It is also very useful in breaking out of an opponent's grip as the hand is slid around the opponent's wrist or arm while this hard point is applied.

PROXIMAL PHALANGES

The knuckles used in punches are the top end of the proximal phalanges. These bones are hard, very near the surface and have no nerve endings. However, they are not well supported by the surrounding bones in the hand and must be applied in the manner shown in Chapter 5, "Strikes and Kicks," to avoid not only damaging the phalanges but also damaging all or some of the other bones in the hand. Overuse and especially misuse of these bones will eventually result in arthritis.

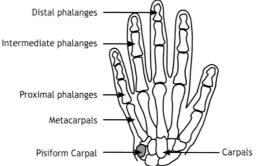

The hardpoints of the hand.

TIBIA

The tibia is one of the biggest and strongest bones in the body and the shin side of the bone is very close to the surface. However it is only the top part of the tibia, the tuberosity of the tibia, which has no nerve endings between it and the surface of the skin. This area is not commonly used by karateka but it is very effective, especially for blocking a *mae-geri-gedan* and *chudan* and also for blocking *mawashi-geri-chudan* and *gedan*. It will seriously injury an attacker and even when practicing this block in class, do so with minimum force. The lower part of the tibia, or the shin as it is commonly known, is relatively sensitive and needs much conditioning before it can be used against hard targets or attacks.

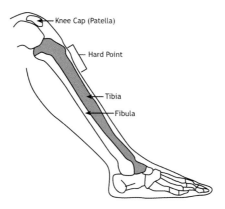

The hardpoints of the leg.

BONES OF THE FEET

These bones are not very strong and are not well supported and so *mawashi-geris* should not be used against hard extremities of an opponent such as those listed above. Rather, these kicks should focus on the back, spine, rib cage, jaw line, neck (front, side and back), thigh, groin or stomach. Never use the feet bones against the cranium, ulna or tibia. None of the many bones of the feet are hard points. However, *karateka* tend to use their feet often and it is important that they use their feet carefully.

Using the feet on a soft target.

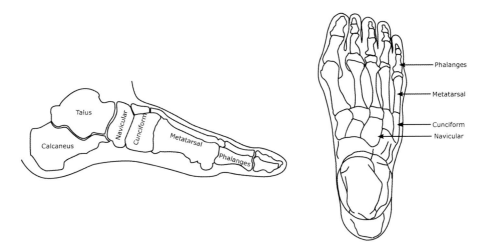

The bones of the feet.

*Proper **gedan-uke** form.*

CHAPTER 13

PRESSURE POINTS

Most karateka do not aim their punches, kicks, blocks, take-downs and weapons correctly. They are simply happy to connect with a general area. If, for example, they are told to perform a *chudan* kick, they are happy to connect anywhere on the torso, not realizing that certain areas of the torso are a lot more vulnerable than others.

To maximize the effectiveness of karate techniques, a knowledge of the body's pressure points is essential.

Effective use of pressure points allows the karateka to not only severely injure an opponent but to also disrupt the opponent's balance, distract the opponent and/or cause the opponent severe discomfort and pain which then allows the karateka to take total control of the opponent.

APPLICATION

Every block, kick, strike, takedown—just about every time you touch an opponent—you should be coming into direct contact with a pressure point. Accurately striking a pressure point is not easy and takes many years of practice. When performing a kata, you are simply going through the motions of connecting with an opponent's pressure points.

Connecting with pressure points not only causes a lot of pain but it can also be very dangerous to the opponent. Pressure point techniques should not be practiced on:

- Persons beyond middle age.
- Persons with high blood pressure.
- Persons on heart medication or muscle relaxants.
- Persons recovering from serious illness or surgery.

Application of pressure point techniques can result in a heart attack or stroke and it is for this reason that the previously mentioned persons should not be used for practice.

*Proper **gedan-uke** form.*

Gedan-uke *impacting on the femoral nerve.*

When practicing in a dojo with a partner remember to:

- Apply pressure gradually, this way you will determine a partner's threshold and be able to stop before you hurt them.
- Not apply pressure point techniques to the same person for more than a few minutes each half hour and do not attack the same pressure point more than three times.
- Immediately release a partner when they indicate submission by tapping their hand.

Yoi *posture.*

Applying pressure to radial and ulna nerves.

LOCATION OF PRESSURE POINTS

There are over one hundred pressure points that can be effectively used by a martial artist.

Some pressure points are found easily and others not. The eyes, larynx and groin are easy to find and when struck effectively will completely disable an opponent. However, a karateka may not want to, or, may not be able to connect with these points, in which case there are many others. By striking the lesser-known points first a karateka may then create access to these three primary pressure points.

The diagrams on the following pages list some of the pressure points that may be used by a karateka.

PRESSURE POINT DIAGRAMS

Please note that the red or yellow shading indicates the high or medium pain levels respectively that are caused when pressure is applied to these points. Pressure points that cause low levels of pain have not been included.

1. Front of Face

	PRESSURE POINT	NERVE/ MUSCLE	COMMENTS
1.1	Eyes		One of the top four most effective pressure points. A hard strike with a single finger or sustained pressure will cause total incapacitation.
1.2	Tip of nose	Nasal nerve	Injury causes tears which in turn causes very temporary incapacitation in the form of blindness.
1.3	Chin	Mertalis	A good strike can jolt the head and neck nerves sufficiently to cause concussion.
1.4	Philtrum	Infraorbital base of nose	Injury causes tears, which in turn causes very temporary incapacitation in the form of blindness.

2. Side of Face

PRESSURE POINT		NERVE/ MUSCLE	COMMENTS
2.1	Temple		A good strike can jolt the head and neck sufficiently to cause concussion or unconsciousness.
2.2	Side of jaw		A good strike can jolt the head and neck sufficiently to cause concussion.
2.3	Under jaw	Auricular, hypoglossal, vagus	A good strike can jolt the head and neck sufficiently to cause concussion.
2.4	Lower jaw bone	Vagus nerve	A good strike can jolt the head and neck sufficiently to cause concussion.
2.5	Larynx	Vagus, cervical, cardiac	One of the top four most effective pressure points. A hard strike with a single finger or sustained pressure will cause total incapacitation.
2.6	Neck artery	Phrenic	Sustained pressure will cause total incapacitation.

3. Back of head

PRESSURE POINT		NERVE/ MUSCLE	COMMENTS
3.1	Center of neck, C2	Accessory nerve, trapezius muscle	The beloved karate chop in the old movies usually focused on this point.
3.2	Whitney's notch	Accessory nerve, trapezius muscle	
3.3	Rear of neck on trapezius	Accessory nerve, trapezius muscle	

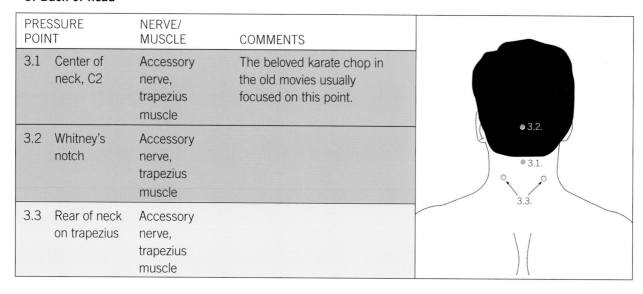

4. Torso and Shoulders

PRESSURE POINT		NERVE/ MUSCLE	COMMENTS	
4.1	Front of shoulders	Axillary nerve, pectoralis minor muscle	A hard strike will cause temporary and limited incapacitation.	
4.2	Jugular notch	Supraclavicular nerve	One of the top four most effective pressure points. A hard strike with a single finger or sustained pressure will cause total incapacitation.	
4.3	Zyphoid process		A hard strike will cause temporary and limited incapacitation due to loss of breath. However this area may be conditioned to take strikes and so resist a strike better.	
4.4	Solar plexus		A hard strike will cause temporary and limited incapacitation. However this may be conditioned to take strikes and so resist a strike better.	
4.5	Floating ribs	Intercostal nerve	A hard strike will can crack or damage these ribs which causes severe pain both immediately and for many weeks.	
4.6	Saiki tanden		A hard strike will cause temporary and limited incapacitation. However this area may be conditioned to take strikes and so resist a strike better.	
4.7	Femoral artery	Femoral nerve		
4.8	Collarbone	Brachial plexus		
4.9	Groin/crotch	Prostate nerve	One of the top four most effective pressure points. A hard strike with a single finger or sustained pressure will cause total incapacitation.	

5. Inside Arm and Armpit

	PRESSURE POINT	NERVE/ MUSCLE	COMMENTS
5.1	Armpit	Brachial plexus nerve	A strong upward thrust with fingers into the armpit causes severe but temporary pain.
5.2	Middle of inside elbow	Median nerve	
5.3	Base of bicep tendon	Radial and median nerves	
5.4	1/3 down the bottom of forearm	Ulnar nerve	
5.5	1/4 down top of forearm	Radial nerve	
5.6	Wrist	Median nerve	
5.7	Wrist	Ulnar nerve	
5.8	Wrist joint	Ulnar nerve	
5.9	Wrist joint	Radial nerve	

6. Outside Arm and Hand

	PRESSURE POINT	NERVE/ MUSCLE	COMMENTS
6.1	Upper arm	Radial nerve, tricep brachi muscle	
6.2	Elbow–outside	Ulnar nerve	The "funny bone." Brief incapacitation if struck hard.
6.3	1/3 down outside forearm	Radial and musculocutaneous nerves	
6.4	Valley between fingers	Radial nerve between thumb and 1st finger and 2nd finger; 1st and digital nerve between 2nd and 3rd finger; ulnar nerve between 3rd and 4th finger.	

7. Inside Leg

PRESSURE POINT		NERVE/ MUSCLE	COMMENTS
7.1	Instep	Deep peroneal nerve	A hard and successful strike can cause immediate destabilization of an opponent.
7.2	Above ankle bone	Tibial nerve	A hard and successful strike can cause immediate destabilization of an opponent.
7.3	Achilles tendon	Tibial nerve	A hard and successful strike can cause immediate destabilization of an opponent.
7.4	Base of calf	Tibial	A hard and successful strike can cause immediate destabilization of an opponent.
7.5	Base of kneecap	Saphenous nerve	A hard and successful strike can cause immediate destabilization of an opponent.
7.6	Rear of knee	Tibial and saphenous nerve	A hard and successful strike can cause immediate destabilization of an opponent.
7.7	2/3 down rear of thigh	Sciatic nerve	A hard and successful strike can cause immediate destabilization of an opponent.
7.8	Inside knee joint	Popliteal	A hard and successful strike can cause immediate destabilization of an opponent.

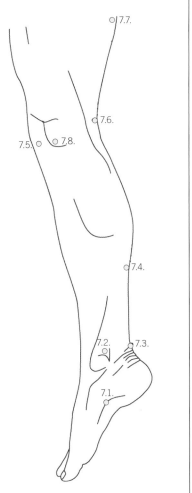

8. Outside leg

PRESSURE POINT		NERVE/ MUSCLE	COMMENTS
8.1	Above ankle bone	Superficial peroneal nerve	A hard and successful strike can cause immediate destabilization of an opponent.
8.2	Outside knee joint	Sciatic nerve	A hard and successful strike can cause total and immediate destabilization of an opponent. Not only is the nerve injured but the ligaments are torn and the leg is no longer able to support itself.
8.3	Outside thigh	Femoral nerve	A hard and successful strike can cause immediate destabilization of an opponent. This is a favorite target in Mixed Martial Arts, Kick-boxing and Tae Kwon Do as it is a relatively easy target.

9. Top of foot

PRESSURE POINT		NERVE/ MUSCLE
9.1	Valley between big and 1st toe	Deep peroneal

10. Back

PRESSURE POINT		NERVE/ MUSCLE
10.1	Rear shoulder midway between neck and shoulder joint	Cranial nerve; upper trapezius muscle
10.2	Trapezius rhomboid	Dorsal scapular nerve; muscles
10.3	Just below ribs	Lateral cutaneous nerve
10.4	Kidneys	Thoracic nerve

CHAPTER 14

TRAINING AIDS

TRADITIONAL TRAINING AIDS

Chi Shi (Weighted Poles)

Chi shi are concrete or stone weights attached to a wooden pole. The karateka grips the unweighted end of the wooden pole and moves wrist and arms in motions used in techniques normally used in kata or kumite. This weighted training helps strengthen the fingers, hands, arms, and chest. *Chi shi* can vary in weight depending on the practitioner's size and strength.

Chi shi *(weighted poles)*

Tetsu Geta (Iron Clogs)

Tetsu geta are worn on the feet and gripped with toes. This gripping is necessary to prevent the sandals from falling off. The karateka then performs kata or kicks. This strengthens the legs.

Ishi Sashi (Hand Weights)

Ishi sashi are hand-held weights in the shape of padlocks that are traditionally made of stone but today are made of iron. As with *chi shi* the karateka performs kata or kumite while holding these. Aggressive moves will cause the *ishi sashi* to move in the hands unless they are gripped strongly. *Ishi sashi* will strengthen hands, wrists, arms and chest.

Ishi sashi *(hand weights)*

Makiage Kigu (Twisting Sticks)

The *makiage kigu* is a weight hanging by a rope from a wooden handle. The karateka grasps the handle with the weight hanging in the middle, and twists the handle to wrap the rope around the handle. The weight is raised and lowered through the twisting to strengthen the wrists. Use of the *makiage kigu* are very good for strengthening hands and wrists.

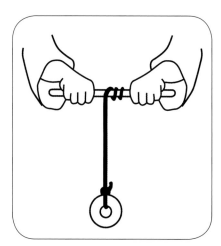

Makiage kigu *(twisting sticks)*

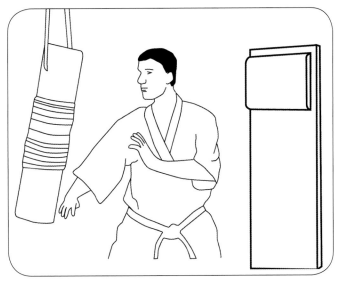

Makiwara *(striking poles or planks)*

Makiwara (Striking Poles or Planks)

There are two types of *makiwara,* the first, *tachi-makiwara* is the most common and is attached to the ground. The second type is the *sage-makiwara,* which is hung from the roof or from a wall bracket and looks like a wooden punching bag with padding around the middle.

The *tachi-makiwara* comes in two forms, one flat and the other round. The flat *makiwara* is created with a board placed into the ground and some type of padding on the top. The padding is about thirty centimeters long and twelve centimeters wide. The practitioner stands in front of the *makiwara* and strikes the padded section. The round *makiwara* is also embedded into the ground but allows the karateka to strike or kick it from all sides.

Yari Bako (Sand Bowl)

The *yari bako* is simply a bowl filled with fine sand into which the karateka strikes with an open hand. This not only strengthens the hands but also conditions the fingers and fingertips.

Nigiri Game (Gripping Jars)

Nigiri game are ceramic jars filled with sand. The lip of the jars has a rim of about one finger-width and the mouth of the jar is as wide as the palm of the hand. The jars are gripped around a lipped rim and the karateka lifts them off the ground and moves about. This strengthens the fingers, arms, shoulders, back, and legs.

Nigiri game *(gripping jars)*

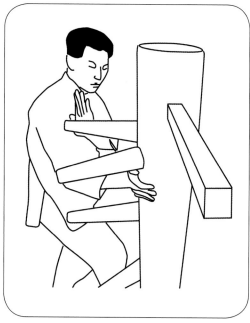

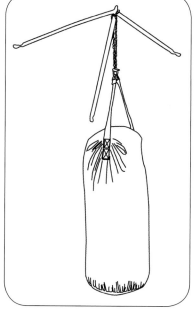

Wooden dummy

Punching bag

Wooden Dummy

The wooden dummy is generally associated with kung fu but is also an excellent training aid for karate. They are usually made from a hard wood such as rosewood and are well polished to prevent splinters.

As the trainee repeatedly strikes and blocks on the hard wood these training aids greatly assist with body conditioning.

MODERN TRAINING AIDS

Punching Bag

Punching bags come in a variety of shapes, sizes and weights. They are usually hung from the roof of the dojo or from a bracket attached to the wall. A punching bag should be at least 25 kg/55 lbs for children and 50 kg/110 lbs for adults. The punching bags are usually made from canvas and stuffed with anything from sawdust to paper to sand. Hard, repetitive punching will result in the loss of skin from the knuckles even while wearing gloves. However, repetitive training will ensure that the knuckles become calloused.

The lowest point of the punching bag should be at groin height and the highest point should be in-line with the top of the head. The heavier the punching bag, the less it will move while punching and kicking.

Punching bags can be used to train for speed, power and combinations of attacks.

Speed Ball

As with a punching bag, a speed ball is attached to the roof or to a wall mounted bracket and is set at head height. It is used exclusively for punching and is designed to develop speed and coordination.

Touch or Jab Pads

These are similar to gloves except they are held in an open hand with a large flat surface where an opponent can practice his punching while the wearer of the pads moves his hands to create a moving target. These pads are very effective for accuracy training.

The pads may also be held next to the head allowing an opponent to practice *mawashi* kicks.

Tetami

These are floor mats that are used during *kumite* competitions. They provide a safe, non-slip surface on which to fight. The mats are generally about 8m x 8m but can be as big as 12m x 12m. They are about 3cm thick and are made of high-density foam.

They are often purchased in segments of about a 1m x 1m that have jigsaw-like edges that hold the pieces together.

Striking Pad

Striking pads are large and thick and are used for strength and power training. The pads usually come with straps on one side where the assistant can secure the pad. These are probably the best training aids for kicks as the assistant is able to keep the pad steady and allow the trainee to perform quick, fast and hard repetitive kicks to *chudan*, *gedan* and *jodan* levels.

Touch or jab pads

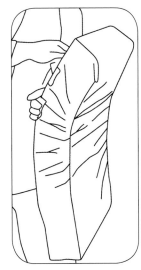

Striking pad

CHAPTER 15

KOBUDO

Kobudo is a separate form of martial arts and as such, should have its own manual. However, because *kobudo* is practiced by many karateka it has been included here. *Kubudo* has its own grading system and *kobudo* students wear a brown gi. Belts from yellow to brown have a black stripe down the middle.

Kobudo is the Okinawan art of weapons use. As Okinawans were not permitted to carry weapons for hundreds of years, they taught themselves how to use everyday tools as weapons.

Kobudo improves the flow of body movement and increases coordination, especially hand-eye coordination. Apart from coordination, *kobudo* also increases an individual's strength as the weapons can weigh up to three kilograms or six and a half pounds.

KAMA

The *Kama* was originally used for cutting grass or sugar cane, and was the only bladed farm implement allowed by the occupiers of Okinawa. It is a close-range weapon. It is still used as a tool in Okinawa today and may be purchased at a hardware store.

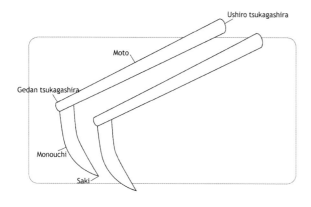

Kama

Kama *in action.*

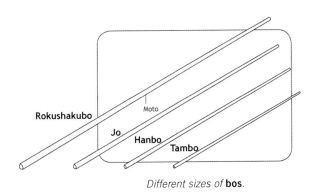

Different sizes of **bos**.

Rokushakubo *in action.*

BO

The *bo* is thought to be derived from a walking stick or from the *tenbib,* a wooden staff that was slung across the shoulders to carry a bucket of water at each end. The most common *bo* is the *rokushakubo. Bos* vary in length from 2.5m to 50cm.

Rokushakubo

This is the longest of the *bos.* Originally, it may have been a walking stick or used to carry items over the back. Length: approximately 1.8m.

Jo

A *jo* is a long, wooden staff that is slightly shorter than the *bo.* Length: between 1.27m to 1.4m. Ideally it should be the same length as the height of the user's armpit above the ground.

Hanbo

A *hanbo* is exactly half the length of a *rokushakubo* and the length of a "standard" walking stick. Length: 90cm.

Tambo

Tambos are typically made from hardwood, but can also be made from bamboo. Length: approximately 50cm.

SAI

The *sai* has always been a weapon and is not an adaptation from a farm or fishing implement. They are believed to have originated in China. *Sai* were used by law enforcement agencies as weapons and restraining gear. *Sai* are between 15 and 20 inches long and are primarily defensive weapons. Two or even three *sai* were carried, the third being used as a throwing weapon.

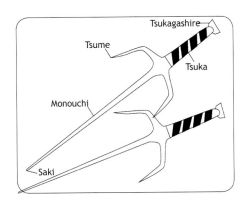

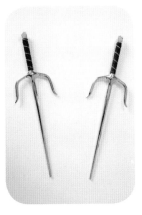

Sai

Sai *in action.*

TONFA

The *tonfa* were originally millstone handles to provide leverage when pushing. An effective defensive and offensive weapon, *tonfa* are used by police world-wide. Length: 50cm to 60cm.

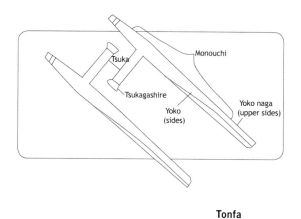

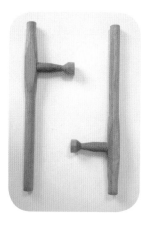

Tonfa

Tonfa *in action.*

NUNCHAKU

Used for thrashing grain or as a horse bit, *nunchaku* were made famous by Bruce Lee. The link between each wooden section can be made from rope or chain. The length of each stick should be approximatly 60cm.

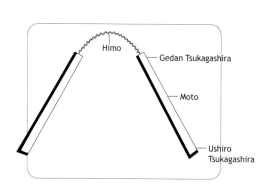

Nunchaku

Nunchaku *with rope* **himo.**

Nunchaku *with chain* **himo.**

Nunchaku *in action.*

EKKU

This is a boat oar put to fighting use by Okinawan fishermen. Its use is similar to that of a *bo* except for the blade. The blade is also used to flick sand into an opponent's eyes. Length: 1.6m

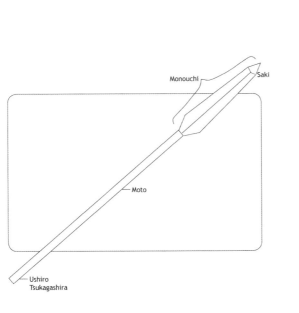

Ekku

Ekku *in action.*

TANTO

The *tanto* is a common Japanese single or, occasionally, double-edged knife. The blade length is 15cm to 30cm.

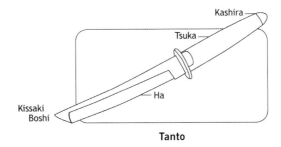

Tanto

KATANA

The *katana* is a curved, sharp, single-edged sword. Length: 70cm to 90cm—traditionally, the blade length was selected by having the recipient stand up straight, hold the sword naturally and swing his arm down at his side. If the length is correct, the blade tip should just clear the ground without touching it.

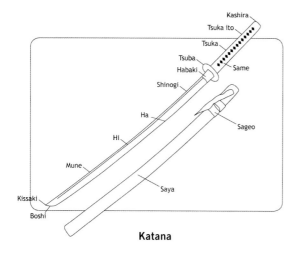

Katana

Kama *versus* **bo**.

Bo *versus* **tonfa**.

Bo *versus* **bo**.

Kama *versus* **bo**.

CHAPTER 16

DOJO LANGUAGE

JAPANESE TO ENGLISH

A

Age	Rising
Age uke	Rising block
Age zuki	Rising punch
Ago	Chin
Ago geri	Chin kick
Aiuchi	Simultaneous scoring techniques (competition)
Akka no kachi	Red wins (competition)
Ao no kachi	Blue wins (competition)
Ashi	Foot/leg
Ashi barai	Foot sweep
Ashi guruma	Leg wheel
Ashi hishigi	Leg crush
Ashi kubi	Ankle
Ashi kubi hishigi	Ankle crush
Ashi waza	Foot techniques
Atama	Head
Atama uchi	Strike with head
Ate waza	Smashing techniques
Atemi	Striking
Atemi waza	Striking techniques

B

Barai	Sweep
Bo	Staff (long-range weapon)
Bojitsu	Staff techniques
Boshi	Curved edge
Budo	Martial way
Bujutsu	Fighting arts of the warrior class of Japan
Bunkai	Application of a kata
Bushi	Warrior class of Japan
Bushido	Way of the warrior

C

Chishi	Weighted poles (training aid)
Choku	Straight
Choku zuki	Straight punch
Chuan fa	Fist way
Chudan	Middle (of body, i.e. torso)
Chudan mae geri	Front kick to body
Chudan uke	Middle block
Chudan zuki	Middle punch

D

Dachi	Stance
Dan 段	Rank of black belt; first *dan* is the lowest, tenth is the highest
Dan zuki	Consecutive punch
De ashi barai	Forward foot sweep
Denzook	No count
Do	The way
Dojo 道場	Exercise hall, the place where one practices the martial arts
Domo arigato	Thank you very much

E

Ekku	Oar (weapon)
Empi	Elbow
Empi uchi	Elbow strike

F

Fudo dachi	Rooted stance
Fumikomi	Stamping kick

G

Ganmen	Face
Ganmen uchi	Facial strike
Gari	Reap
Gasshuku	Training camp
Gatame	Arm bar hold
Geashi	Reversal
Gedan	Lower, waist or below
Gedan barai	Low block
Gedan juji uke	Lower cross block
Gedan shuto uke	Lower knife-hand block
Geri	Kick
Gi 着	Uniform for practicing martial arts
Go	Hard; five
Gohon uchi	Five-finger strike
Goshi	Hip throw
Gozai imasu	Much (past)
Gozai mashita	Much (present)
Guruma	Wheel-like throw
Gyaku	Reverse or reversal
Gyaku mawashi geri	Reverse roundhouse kick
Gyaku juji jime	Reverse cross choke
Gyaku zuki	Reverse punch (opposite hand & leg)

H

Ha	Edge
Habaki	Blade collar
Hachi	Eight
Hachiji dachi	Open leg stance
Hachimachi	Towel used as a headband
Hadake	Naked
Hadake jime	Naked choke
Hadari	Left
Hai	Yes
Hai wan	Back arm
Haishu	Back of the hand
Haishu uchi	Backhand strike
Haisoku	Instep
Haisoku geri	Instep kick
Haitto	Ridgehand (first knuckle of the thumb and the side of the hand)
Haitto uchi	Ridgehand strike
Hajimae	Begin
Hamon	Edge pattern
Hane	Spring
Hane goshi	Spring hip throw
Hane makikomi	Springing winding throw
Hangetsu dachi	Hourglass stance
Hanshi	Instructor, head person of a style
Hansoku	Disqualification (competition)
Hansoku Chui	*Nihon* penalty (competition)
Hara	Muscular core of body
Hara tsurikomi ashi	Lift pull sweep
Harai	Sweep
Harai goshi	Sweep hip throw
Hasami zuki	Scissors punch
Hata	Flag of the club
Heiko dachi	Parallel stance
Heiko zuki	Simultaneous double punch
Heisoku dachi	Attention Stance
Heiwan uchi	Forearm strike
Hi	Groove
Hidari	Left (side)
Hiji	Elbow
Hiji-ate	Elbow strike
Hiji-uchi	Elbow strike
Hikiwake	Draw (competition)
Hiraken	Fore-knuckle fist
Hiraken zuki	Fore-knuckle punch
Hishigi	Crush
Hittsui	Knee

Hittsui geri	Knee strike (upward, side)
Hizagashira	Kneecap
Hon	Fingers. *See also* Gohon
Honbu	Headquarters

I

Ichi or sho	One
Ippon	One point (competition)
Ippon ken	One knuckle fist
Ippon kumite	One point (sparring)
Ippon seoi nage	One-armed shoulder throw
Irimi waza	Entering technique
Ishi sashi	Hand weights (training aid)

J

Jime	Choke or strangle
Jitsu	Art
Jiyu ippon	One-step sparring
Jiyu kumite	Free sparring
Jo	Short staff
Jodan	Upper, shoulders or above
Jodan mae geri	Upper body kick
Jodan zuki	Upper punch
Jogai	Moved out of arena (competition)
Jo-jitsu	Short staff techniques
Joseke	Upper seat
Ju	Soft; ten
Ju ichi	Eleven
Judo	A martial arts style featuring throwing
Judoka	Practitioner of judo
Juji	Cross
Juji gatame	Arm bar, cross-body and through legs and across hips
Juji uke	Cross block

K

Kagi zuki	Hook punch
Kakato	Heel
Kake	Application of the technique
Kake uke	Hook block
Kakiwake uke	Pushing through block
Kakuto uke	Bent wrist block
Kama	Sickle
Kamae	Fighting stance

Kami shio gatame	Upper four-corner hold
Kan	House
Kanji	Japanese writing
Kansetsu	Joint lock
Kansetsu waza	Joint-locking techniques
Kara	Empty
Karate 空手	Martial arts style featuring strikes
Karate do	The way of karate
Karateka	A practitioner of karate
Kashira	Pommel
Kata	Stylized form, pre-arranged techniques
Katame	Grappling
Katame waza	Grappling and ground-fighting techniques
Katana	Long sword
Katate tori	Grasping of hands
Katsu	Revival techniques
Kazuri kesa gatame	Modified scarf hold
Keage	Snap
Keiko	Training
Keikoku	One-point penalty (competition)
Keito	Wrist, chicken head
Kekomi	Thrust
Kempo	Fist way
Kendo	Japanese sword fighting
Kensetsu geri	Kick, stamping at foot joint in leg
Kentsui	Hammer fist
Kentsui uchi	Hammer fist strike
Keri	Kicking
Keri ashi	Kicking foot
Keri waza	Kicking technique
Kesa gatame	Scarf hold
Kesa geri	Diagonal kick
Ki 気合	Vital energy
Kiai	Shout or yell with vital energy (*ki*)
Kiba dachi	Horse stance
Kihon	Basic technique
Kime	Focus of the *ki*
Kin geri	Groin kick
Kissaki	Point
Kitskay	Attention
Kizami zuki	Jab
Ko	Minor
Kodokan	Headquarters of judo in Japan
Kohai	Student, junior to oneself
Ko uchi	Bent wrist strike

Ko uke	Wrist or arch block	*Maki*	Wrapping
Koken	Wrist joint	*Maki geashi*	Wrapping reversal
Koko uchi	Tiger mouth strike	*Makiage kiga*	Twisting sticks (training aid)
Kokutsu dachi	Back stance	*Makiwara*	Striking pole or plank (training aid)
Komi	Pulling	*Matae*	Stop
Konban wa	Good evening (after dark)	*Matte*	Wait
Konnichi wa	Good evening (daylight hours)	*Mawaru*	Turn around
Kosa dachi	Cross-legged stance	*Mawashi geri*	Roundhouse kick
Koshi	Hip; ball of foot	*Mawashi uke*	Roundhouse block
Koshi guruma	Hip wheel throw	*Mawashi zuki*	Roundhouse punch
Koshi jime	Hip choke	*Mawat te*	Turn around
Koshi waza	Hip technique	*Mienai*	View obscured (competition)
Koshin	Rearward	*Migi*	Right (side)
Kosoto gakae	Minor outer hook	*Mikazuki*	Crescent
Kosoto gari	Minor outer reaping throw	*Mikazuki geri*	Crescent kick
Kouchi gari	Minor inner reaping throw	*Mikazuki geri uke*	Crescent kick block
Ku	Nine	*Mo Ichido*	Once again
Kubi	Neck	*Mokuso*	Silent contemplation
Kumade	Bare hand	*Moro*	Augmented
Kumikata	Methods of holding	*Moro ubi tori*	Augmented finger pull
Kumite 組手	Sparring or coming together of hands	*Morote*	Two-arm or two-hand
Kusarigama	Sickle with a rope or chain attached	*Morote seoi nage*	Two-arm shoulder throw
Kusho	Vital points of the body	*Morote uke*	Double-forearm block
Kuzushi	Unbalancing (eight directions)	*Morote zuki*	Double-forward-fist strike
Kyoshi	Instructor, master	*Mudansha*	Non-black belt holder
Kyu	Grade under black belt; tenth *kyu* is the lowest and first is the highest	*Mune*	Chest; back of blade
		Muni gatame	Chest hold
Kyusho	Pressure point	*Mushin*	Mind of no mind
Kyusho jitsu	The art of manipulating pressure points	*Musubi-dachi*	Stance with heels together and feet pointing outward

M

Ma	Distance between opponents		
Ma ai	Distance		
Mae	Front		
Mae ashi kekomi	Front leg thrust		
Mae ashi geri	Front leg kick		
Mae empi uchi	Forward elbow strike		
Mae geri	Front kick		
Mae geri keage	Front snap kick		
Mae geri kekomi	Front thrust kick		
Mae hiji ate	Forward elbow strike		
Mae tobi geri	Kick, jumping front		
Mae ukemi	Fall/roll forward		
Maete	Jab		
Maitta	I give up		

N

Nagashi uke	Flowing block
Nage	Throwing
Nage no kata	Formalized throw
Nage waza	Throwing technique
Naginata	Halberd used by Japanese women
Naihanshi-dachi	Stance with the feet apart, toes pointing inward
Nakadaka ippon ken	Fist with middle finger knuckle protruding
Nakazato, Shugoro	*Shorin-ryu* grandmaster
Nami juji jime	Normal cross choke
Ne waza	Ground fighting techniques
Necho	Cat
Necho ashi dachi	Cat stance

Ni	Two
Ni ju	Twenty
Ni ju ichi	Twenty-one
Nidan	Second black belt
Nidan geri	Double jumpkick
Nihon	Two points competition)
Nihon nukite	Two-finger spearhand
Nihon zuki	Double punch
Nigiri game	Gripping jars—training aid
Nukite	Spearhand
Nunchaku	Flail-like weapon of two rods joined by rope or chain

O

O goshi	Major hip throw
O guruma	Major wheel throw
Obi 帯	Belt
Ohiyo gozaimasu	Good morning
Ohten	Barrel roll
Ohten gatame	Barrel roll arm bar
Oi zuki	Forward lunge punch (same side hand and leg)
Okinawa te	Okinawan hand
Okuri	Sliding
Okuri ashi barai	Foot sweep
Okuri ashi harai	Sliding foot sweep
Okuri eri jime	Sliding collar choke
Onegai shimasu	Please teach me
Oroshi zuki	Descending punch
Osae komi	Hold-down
Osae komi waza	Hold-down techniques
Osoto gari	Major outer reaping throw
Osoto guruma	Major outer wheel throw
Osu	Greeting
Otoshi	Drop
Ouchi gari	Major inner reaping throw
Oyasumi nasai	Good night (upon departing)

R

Randori	Judo-style free sparring
Rei	Bow
Renshi	Instructor—very good (fifth and sixth dan)
Renzoku geri	Combination kick
Roku	Six
Ryu	Style of school or martial art
Ryukyu	Rope Islands

S

Sageo	Hanging cord
Sai	Three-pronged metal weapon
Saiken tanden	Source of the ki
Sakotsu	Collarbone
Sakotsu shuto	Collarbone knife-hand
Same	Ray skin
San	Three
San ju	Thirty
Sanbon zuki	Three-punch combination
Sanchin dachi	Hourglass stance (derived from Sanchin kata)
Sasae (tsuri komi) ashi	Lifting pulling foot block
Saya	Scabbard
Seiken	Fore fist
Seiryuto	Ox-jaw hand
Seiryuto-uke	Ox-jaw block
Seiza	Sitting position
Sempai	Senior
Sensei 先生	Teacher
Seoi	Shoulder
Shi	Four
Shiai	Contest
Shichi	Seven
Shihan	Instructor, master instructor (fourth through fifth dan)
Shiho	Four corners, or all directions
Shiho nage	Throw, all directions
Shiko dachi	Stance with feet apart, toes angled out
Shime	Choke
Shime waza	Choking techniques
Shimpan	Referee in a match
Shinogi	Blade ridge
Shiro	White
Shizentai	Natural posture stance
Shomen	The front
Shotei	Palm heel strike
Shotei uke	Palm heel block
Shu wan	Palm arm
Shuto	Knife-edge hand (little finger side of palm)
Shuto uchi	Knife hand strike
Shuto uke	Knife hand block
Sode	Sleeve
Sode tsuri	Sleeve lifting pulling hip throw

komi goshi	
Sokko	Ridge of foot
Sokuto	Edge of foot
Sokuto keage	Kick that snaps with the edge of the foot
Soto	Outside (of opponent's stance)
Soto age uke	Outer upper block
Soto makikomi	Outer winding throw
Soto mikazui geri	Outer crescent kick
Soto shuto	Outside knife-hand block
Soto ude uke	Outside forearm block
Suki	Opening
Sukui nage	Scooping throw
Sumea gaeshi	Corner reversal
Sumi otoshi	Corner drop
Sunbon	Three points (competition)
Sute	Sacrifice
Sutemi	Roll
Sutemi waza	Sacrifice techniques

T

Tachi waza	Standing throwing techniques
Tai	Body
Tai otoshi	Body drop
Tai sabaki	Body movement
Tameshiwari	Breaking demonstration
Tan den	Muscular core of body
Tani otoshi	Valley drop
Tanto	Short sword
Tate empi uchi	Upward elbow strike
Tate hiji ate	Upward elbow strike
Tate zuki	Vertical punch (boxer's jab)
Te waza	Hand techniques
Teiji dachi	T-stance
Teisho	Palm heel
Teisho uchi	Palm heel strike
Teisho uke	Palm heel block
Tekubi	Wrist
Tekubi tori	Wrist pull
Tetsu geta	Iron dogs (training aid)
Tettsui	Hammer fist; downward strike with closed fist, little finger side as the striking surface
Tobi keri	Flying front kick
Tobi yoko geri	Jumping side kick
Tome	Return to original position

Tomoe nage	Stomach throw
Tonfa	Wooden rod with handle at right angle, used in pairs (weapon)
Toranai	No points (tournament)
Tori	Defender, demonstrator of a technique; pull
Torimasen	Unacceptable as scoring technique (competition)
Tsuba	Guard
Tsuka	Handle
Tsuka ito	Cord wrap
*Tsuki 突き	Punch; knuckle strike with first two knuckles only
Tsuki waza	Punching techniques
Tsukuri	Stepping into the throw
Tsuri	Lifting
Tsuri goshi	Lifting hip throw
Tsuri komi goshi	Lifting pulling hip throw
Tuite	Grappling
Tzuzukete	Resume fighting/begin (competition)

U

Uchi	Inner; or, strike
Uchi mata	Inner thigh throw
Uchi mawashi geri	Inside roundhouse kick
Uchi waza	Striking techniques
Uchideshi	Special disciple
Uchikomi	Repeated practice of throwing techniques
Ude	Forearm
Ude gatame	Forearm arm bar
Ude tori	Forearm pull
Ude uki	Forearm block
Uke	Block (*age uke*); attacker, to whom techniques are done
Ukemi	Falling and rolling exercises
Ukemi waza	Falling technique
Uki	Floating
Uki goshi	Floating hip throw
Uki otoshi	Floating drop
Uki waza	Floating throw
Ura	Back or flip side
Ura nage	Back hip throw
Ura zuki	Back punch; close range uppercut
Uraken	Backfist
Uraken uchi	Backfist strike
Ushiro	Rear

Ushiro ashi geri	Rear leg kick
Ushiro geri	Back Kick
Ushiro goshi	Back hip throw

W

Wakare	Separation
Wan	Arm
Wanto	Sword arm
Washide	Eagle hand
Waza	Technique
Waza ari	Half point in match (WKC)

Y

Yakusoku	Promise to hit
Yama	Mountain
Yama bushi	Mountain warriors
Yama zuki	U-Punch
Yame	Stop
Yari	Spear
Yari bako	Sand bowl (training aid)
Yasume	At ease
Yawara	Control
Yoi 用意	Ready
Yoko	Side
Yoko gake	Side body drop
Yoko geri	Side kick
Yoko otoshi	Side drop
Yoko shio gatame	Side four corner hold
Yoko shuto	Side knife-hand
Yoko tobo geri	Jump side kick
Yoko wakare	Side separation
Yoko zuki	Side punch
Yubi	Finger
Yubi tori	Finger pull
Yudansha	One who is a black belt

Z

Zazen	Sitting meditation
Zen	Buddhist sect
Zenkutzo dachi	Forward stance
Zenshin	Forward

* *Tsuki* is generally used as part of a compound word for any one of various punches and virtually never stands alone to describe a discrete technique. When used in a compound word where *tsuki* does not come first its spelling and pronunciation change to "*zuki.*"

ENGLISH TO JAPANESE

A

Ankle	*Ashi kubi*
Ankle crush	*Ashi kubi hishigi*
Application of form	*Bunkai*
Application of the technique	*Kake*
Arm	*Wan*
Arm bar, barrel roll	*Ohten gatame*
Arm bar, cross-body, through legs and across hips	*Juji gatame*
Arm bar, forearm	*Ude gatame*
Arm bar, straight, with wrist on opponent's elbow	*Juji gatame*
At ease	*Yasume*
Attention	*Kitskay*
Augmented	*Moro*

B

Back arm	*Hai wan*
Back fist	*Uraken*
Back of the hand	*Haishu*
Back or flip side	*Ura*
Ball of foot	*Koshi*
Barrel roll	*Ohten*
Begin	*Hajimae*
Belt	*Obi*
Blade collar	*Habaki*
Blade ridge	*Shinogi*
Block	*Uke*
Block, bent wrist	*Kakuto uke*
Block, crescent kick	*Mikazuki geri uke*
Block, cross	*Juji uke*
Block, double forearm	*Morote uke*
Block, flowing	*Nagashi uke*
Block, forearm	*Ude uki*
Block, hook	*Kake uke*
Block, knifehand	*Shuto uke*
Block, lifting pulling foot	*Sasae (tsuri komi) ashi*
Block, low	*Gedan barai*
Block, lower cross	*Gedan juji uke*
Block, lower knifehand	*Gedan shuto uke*
Block, middle	*Chudan uke*
Block, outer upper	Soto age uke
Block, outside forearm	*Soto ude uke*
Block, outside knifehand	*Soto shuto*
Block, ox-jaw	*Seiryuto-uke*

Block, palm heel	*Shotei uke; teisho uke*
Block, pushing through	*Kakiwake uke*
Block, rising	*Age uke*
Block, roundhouse	*Mawashi uke*
Block, wrist or arch	*Ko uke*
Body	*Tai*
Body movement	*Tai Sabaki*
Bow	*Rei*
Breaking demonstration	*Tameshiwari*
Bridge of foot	*Sokko*
Buddhist sect	*Zen*

C

Camp, training	*Gasshuku*
Cat	*Necho*
Chest	*Mune*
Chest hold	*Muni gatame*
Chin	*Ago*
Chin kick	*Ago geri*
Choke	*Shime*
Choke or strangle	*Jime*
Choke, hip	*Koshi jime*
Choke, naked	*Hadake jime*
Choke, normal cross	*Nami juji jime*
Choke, reverse cross	*Gyaku juji jime*
Choke, sliding collar	*Okuri eri jime*
Close range uppercut	*Ura zuki*
Collarbone	*Sakotsu*
Collarbone knifehand	*Sakotsu shuto*
Competition, blue wins	*Ao no kachi*
Competition, draw	*Hikiwake*
Competition, moved out of arena	*Jogai*
Competition, one point	*Ippon*
Competition, one point penalty	*Keikoku*
Competition, red wins	*Akka no kachi*
Competition, resume fighting/begin	*Tzuzukete hajime*
Competition, scoring techniques	*Aiuchi*
Competition, stop	*Yame*
Competition, three points	*Sunbon*
Competition, two points	*Nihon*
Competition, two points penalty	*Hansoku*
Competition, unacceptable as scoring technique	*Torimasen*

Competition, view obscured	*Mienai*
Contest	*Shiai*
Control	*Yawara*
Cord wrap	*Tsuka ito*
Corner reversal	*Sumea gaeshi*
Crescent	*Mikazuki*
Cross	*Juji*
Crush	*Hishigi*
Curved Edge	*Boshi*

D

Defender, demonstrator of a technique; or, pull	*Tori*
Distance	*Ma ai*
Distance between opponents	*Ma*
Drop	*Otoshi*
Drop, body	*Tai otoshi*
Drop, corner	*Sumi otoshi*
Drop, valley	*Tani otoshi*

E

Eagle hand	*Washide*
Edge of blade	*Ha*
Edge of foot	*Sokuto*
Eight	*Hachi*
Elbow	*Empi; hiji*
Eleven	*Ju ichi*
Empty	*Kara*
Exercise hall, place where one practices martial arts	*Dojo*

F

Face	*Ganmen*
Fall/roll forward	*Mae ukemi*
Falling and rolling exercises	*Ukemi*
Fighting arts of the warrior class of Japan	*Bujutsu*
Finger	*Yubi*
Finger pull	*Yubi tori*
Fingers, *see also Strike, five finger*	*Hon*
Fist way	*Chuan fa or kempo*
Fist, fore-knuckle	*Hiraken*
Fist, hammer	*Kentsui*
Fist, middle finger knuckle protruding	*Nakadaka ippon ken*

Fist, one knuckle	*Ippon ken*
Five	*Go*
Flag of the club	*Hata*
Floating	*Uki*
Floating drop	*Uki otoshi*
Focus	*Kime*
Foot/leg	*Ashi*
Fore fist	*Seiken*
Forearm	*Ude*
Forearm pull	*Ude tori*
Forward	*Zenshin*
Founder of Judo	*Kano, Jigoro*
Four	*Shi*
Four corners, or all directions	*Shiho*
Front	*Mae or shomen*
Front leg thrust	*Mae ashi kekomi*
Full point in a contest	*Ippon*

G

Give up, I	*Maitta*
Good evening (after dark)	*Konban wa*
Good evening (daylight hours)	*Konnichi wa*
Good morning	*Ohiyo gozaimasu*
Good night (upon departing)	*Oyasumi nasai*
Grade under black belt; 10th (lowest) to 1st	*Kyu*
Grandmaster; *Shorin-ryu*	*Nakuzatu, Shugoru*
Grappling	*Katame or tuite*
Grasping of hands	*Katate Tori*
Greeting	*Osu*
Groove of blade	*Hi*
Guard	*Tsuba*

H

Halberd, used by Japanese women	*Naginata*
Half point in match (WKC)	*Waza ari*
Hammer fist; downward strike with closed fist	*Tettsui*
Hand	*Go; Te*
Hand, bare	*Kumade*
Handle	*Tsuka*
Hanging cord	*Sageo*
Head	*Atama*
Headquarters	*Honbu*
Headquarters of judo in Japan	*Kodokan*

Heel	*Kakato*
Hip	*Koshi*
Hold, arm bar	*Gatame*
Hold, modified scarf	*Kazuri kesa gatame*
Hold, scarf	*Kesa gatame*
Hold, upper four-corner	*Kami shio gatame*
Hold-down	*Osae komi*
Holding, methods of	*Kumikata*
Hook, minor outer	*Kosoto gakae*

I

Inner; or, strike	*Uchi*
Instep	*Haisoku*
Instructor—very good (fifth and sixth *dan*)	*Renshi*
Instructor, head person of a style (ninth and tenth *dan*)	*Hanshi*
Instructor, master (seventh and eighth *dan*)	*Kyoshi*
Instructor, master instructor	*Shihan*

J

Jab	*Kizami zuki; maete*

K

Karate, a practitioner of	*Karateka*
Karate, the way of	*Karate-do*
Kick	*Geri*
Kick, back	*Ushiro geri*
Kick, combination	*Renzoku geri*
Kick, crescent	*Mikazuki geri*
Kick, diagonal	*Kesa geri*
Kick, double jump	*Nidan geri*
Kick, flying front	*Tobi keri*
Kick, front	*Mae geri*
Kick, front leg	*Mae ashi geri*
Kick, front snap	*Mae geri keag*
Kick, front thrust	*Mae geri kekomi*
Kick, front to body	*Chudan mae geri*
Kick, groin	*Kin geri*
Kick, inside roundhouse	*Uchi mawashi geri*
Kick, instep	*Haisoku geri*
Kick, jump side	*Yoko tobo geri*
Kick, jumping front	*Mae tobi geri*
Kick, jumping side	*Tobi yoko geri*

Kick, outer crescent	*Soto mikazui geri*
Kick, rear leg	*Ushiro ashi geri*
Kick, reverse roundhouse	*Gyaku mawashi geri*
Kick, roundhouse	*Mawashi geri*
Kick, side	*Yoko geri*
Kick, snap with the edge of the foot	*Sokuto keage*
Kick, stamping	*Fumikomi*
Kick, stamping at foot or joint in leg	*Kensetsu geri*
Kick, upper body	*Jodan mae geri*
Kicking	*Keri*
Kicking foot	*Keri ashi*
Knee	*Hittsui*
Knee cap	*Hizagashira*
Knife-edge hand	*Shuto*

L

Left (side)	*Hidari*
Leg crush	*Ashi hishigi*
Leg wheel	*Ashi guruma*
Lifting	*Tsuri*
Lock, joint	*Kansetsu*
Lower, waist; below	*Gedan*

M

Martial way	*Budo*
Middle (of body, i.e. torso)	*Chudan*
Mind of no mind	*Mushin*
Minor	*Ko*
Mountain	*Yama*
Mountain warriors	*Yama bushi*
Muscular core of body	*Hara; tan den*

N

Naked	*Hadake*
Neck	*Kubi*
Nine	*Ku*
No count	*Denzook*
No points (tournament)	*Toranai*
Non-black belt holder	*Mudansha*

O

Okinawa	*Ryukyu*
Okinawan hand	*Okinawa te*

One	Ichi; sho
One who is a black belt	Yudansha
Once again	Mo ichido
Opening	Suki
Outside (of opponent's stance)	Soto
Ox-jaw hand	Seiryuto

P

Palm arm	Shu wan
Palm heel	Teisho
Please teach me	Onegai shimasu
Point of blade	Kissaki
Point just below the navel	Tanden
Pommel	Kashira
Practitioner of judo	Judoka
Pressure point	Kyusho
Pressure point strikes	Kyusho jitsu
Promise to hit	Yakusoku
Pull, augmented finger	Moro ubi tori
Pull, wrist	Tekubi tori
Pulling	Komi
Punch, back	Ura zuki
Punch, consecutive	Dan zuki
Punch, descending	Oroshi zuki
Punch, double	Nihon zuki
Punch, fore knuckle	Hiraken zuki
Punch, forward lunge (same side hand and leg)	Oi zuki
Punch, hook	Kagi zuki
Punch; knuckle strike with first two knuckles only	Tsuki
Punch, middle	Chudan zuki
Punch, reverse (opposite hand and leg)	Gyaku zuki
Punch, rising	Age zuki
Punch, roundhouse	Mawashi zuki
Punch, scissors	Hasami zuki
Punch, side	Yoko zuki
Punch, simultaneous double	Heiko zuki
Punch, straight	Choku zuki
Punch, three-punch combination	Sanbon zuki
Punch, u-	Yama zuki
Punch, upper	Jodan zuki
Punching board	Makiwara

R

Rank of black belt—first to tenth	Dan
Ray skin	Same
Ready	Yoi
Reap	Gari
Rear	Ushiro
Rearward	Koshin
Referee in a match	Shimpan
Repeated practice of throwing techniques	Uchikomi
Return to original position	Tome
Reversal	Geashi
Reverse, Reversal	Gyaku
Ridgehand (first knuckle of thumb and side of hand)	Haitto
Right (side)	Migi
Rising	Age
Roll	Sutemi

S

Sacrifice	Sute
Scabbard	Saya
Second black belt	Nidan
Senior	Sempai
Separation	Wakare
Seven	Shichi
Short staff	Jo
Short staff techniques	Jo-jitsu
Shoulder	Seoi
Shout or yell with vital energy (ki)	Kiai
Side	Yoko
Side body drop	Yoko gake
Side drop	Yoko otoshi
Side four-corner hold	Yoko shio gatame
Side knife-hand	Yoko shuto
Side separation	Yoko wakare
Silent contemplation	Mokuso
Sitting meditation	Zazen
Sitting position	Seiza
Six	Roku
Sleeve	Sode
Sliding	Okuri
Smash, elbow	Hiji-ate
Snap	Keage
Soft	Ju
Source of the ki	Saiken tanden

Sparring	*Kumite*
Sparring, free	*Jiyu kumite*
Sparring, judo style	*Randori*
Sparring, one point	*Ippon kumite*
Sparring, one step	*Jiyu ippon*
Spear	*Yari*
Spearhand	*Nukite*
Special disciple	*Uchideshi*
Spring	*Hane*
Stance	*Dachi*
Stance, attention	*Heisoku dachi*
Stance, back	*Kokutsu dachi*
Stance, cat	*Necho ashi dachi*
Stance, cross-legged	*Kosa dachi*
Stance, feet apart, toes angled out	*Shiko dachi*
Stance, feet apart, toes pointing in	*Naihanshi-dachi*
Stance, fighting	*Kamae*
Stance, forward	*Zenkutzo dachi*
Stance, heels together, feet pointing outwards	*Musubi-dachi*
Stance, horse	*Kiba dachi*
Stance, hourglass (derived from *Sanchin* kata)	*Sanchin dachi; hangetsu dachi*
Stance, natural posture	*Shizentai*
Stance, open leg	*Hachiji dachi*
Stance, parallel	*Heiko dachi*
Stance, rooted	*Fudo dachi*
Stance, t-	*Teiji dachi*
Stepping into the throw	*Tsukuri*
Stop	*Matae; yame*
Straight	*Choku*
Strike with head	*Atama uchi*
Strike, backfist	*Uraken uchi*
Strike, backhand	*Haishu uchi*
Strike, bent wrist	*Ko uchi*
Strike, double forward fist	*Morote tsuki*
Strike, elbow	*Empi uchi; hiji-uchi*
Strike, facial	*Ganmen uchi*
Strike, five-finger	*Gohon uchi*
Strike, forearm	*Heiwan uchi*
Strike, forward elbow	*Mae empi uchi; mae hiji ate*
Strike, hammer fist	*Kentsui uchi*
Strike, knee (upward, side)	*Hittsui geri*
Strike, knifehand	*Shuto uchi*
Strike, palm heel	*Shotei; teisho uchi*
Strike, ridgehand	*Haitto uchi*

Strike, tiger mouth	*Koko uchi*
Strike, upward elbow	*Tate empi uchi; tate hiji ate*
Striking	*Atemi*
Student, junior to oneself	*Kohai*
Style of school or martial art	*Ryu*
Style, martial arts featuring strikes	*Karate*
Style, martial arts featuring throwing	*Judo*
Stylized form, pre-arranged techniques	*Kata*
Sweep	*Harai*
Sweep, foot	*Okuri ashi barai*
Sweep, forward foot	*De ashi barai*
Sweep, lift pull	*Hara tsurikomi ashi*
Sweep, sliding foot	*Okuri (ashi) harai*
Sword arm	*Wanto*
Sword fighting, Japanese	*Kendo*

T

Teacher	*Sensei*
Technique	*Waza*
Technique, basic	*Kihon*
Technique, entering	*Irimi waza*
Technique, falling	*Ukemi waza*
Technique, hip	*Koshi waza*
Technique, kicking	*Keri waza*
Technique, throwing	*Nage waza*
Techniques, choking	*Shime waza*
Techniques, foot	*Ashi waza*
Techniques, grappling and ground-fighting	*Katame waza*
Techniques, ground-fighting	*Ne waza*
Techniques, hand	*Te waza*
Techniques, hold-down	*Osae komi waza*
Techniques, joint locking	*Kansetsu waza*
Techniques, punching	*Tsuki waza*
Techniques, revival	*Katsu*
Techniques, sacrifice	*Sutemi waza*
Techniques, smashing	*Ate waza*
Techniques, staff (long)	*Bojitsu*
Techniques, standing throwing	*Tachi waza*
Techniques, striking	*Atemi waza; uchi waza*
Ten	*Ju*
Thank you very much (past)	*Domo arigato gozai imasu*

Thank you very much (present)	*Domo arigato goazai mashita*
The way	*Do*
Thirty	*San ju*
Three	*San*
Throw, all directions	*Shiho nage*
Throw, back hip	*Ura nage; ushiro goshi*
Throw, floating	*Uki waza*
Throw, floating hip	*Uki goshi*
Throw, formalized	*Nage no kata*
Throw, hip	*Goshi*
Throw, hip wheel	*Koshi guruma*
Throw, inner thigh	*Uchi mata*
Throw, lifting hip	*Tsuri goshi*
Throw, lifting pulling hip	*Tsuri komi goshi*
Throw, major hip	*O goshi*
Throw, major inner reaping	*Ouchi gari*
Throw, major outer reaping	*Osoto gari*
Throw, major outer wheel	*Osoto guruma*
Throw, major wheel	*O guruma*
Throw, minor inner reaping	*Kouchi gari*
Throw, minor outer reaping	*Kosoto gari*
Throw, one-armed shoulder	*Ippon seoi nage*
Throw, outer winding	*Soto makikomi*
Throw, scooping	*Sukui nage*
Throw, sleeve lifting pulling hip	*Sode tsuri komi goshi*
Throw, spring hip	*Hane goshi*
Throw, springing winding	*Hane makikomi*
Throw, stomach	*Tomoe nage*
Throw, sweep hip	*Harai goshi*
Throw, two-arm shoulder	*Morote seoi nage*
Throw, wheel-like	*Guruma*
Throwing	*Nage*
Thrust	*Kekomi*
Towel used as a headband	*Hachimachi*
Training	*Keiko*
Training aid, gripping jars	*Nigiri game*
Training aid, hand weights	*Ishi sashi*
Training aid, iron dogs	*Testu geta*
Training aid, sand bowl	*Yari bako*
Training aid, striking pole or plank	*Makiwara*
Training aid, twisting sticks	*Makiage kigu*
Training aid, weighted poles	*Chishi*
Turn around	*Mawaru; mawat te*
Twenty	*Ni ju*
Twenty-one	*Ni ju ichi*

Two	*Ni*
Two-arm; two-hand	*Morote*
Two-finger spearhand	*Nihon nukite*

U

Unbalancing (eight directions)	*Kuzushi*
Uniform for practicing martial arts	*Gi*
Upper, shoulders; above	*Jodan*
Upper seat	*Joseke*

V

Vertical punch (boxer's jab)	*Tate tsuki*
Vital energy	*Ki*
Vital points of the body	*Kusho*

W

Wait	*Matte*
Warrior class of Japan	*Bushi*
Way of the warrior	*Bushido*
Weapon, flail-like, composed of two rods joined by rope or chain	*Nunchaku*
Weapon, handles for grinding stone, used in pairs	*Tonfa*
Weapon, long sword	*Katana*
Weapon, oar	*Ekku*
Weapon, short sword	*Tanto*
Weapon, sickle	*Kama*
Weapon, sickle with a rope or chain attached	*Kusarigama*
Weapon, staff (long)	*Bo*
Weapon, three-pronged metal weapon	*Sai*
Weapon, threshing tool	*Nunchuku*
White	*Shiro*
Wrapping	*Maki*
Wrapping reversal	*Maki geashi*
Wrist	*Tekubi*
Wrist joint	*Koken*
Wrist, chicken head	*Keito*
Writing, Japanese	*Kanji*

Y

Yes	*Hai*

Arm and abdomen conditioning.

CHAPTER 17

BODY CONDITIONING

CONDITIONING THE CORE

Perhaps the single most important part of the human body, as far as martial artists are concerned, is the core. In Chinese it is known as *dantian* or *tant'ien*, in Japanese it is known as *tanden* or *hara,* in Korean as *danjeon* and in Thai as *dantian.* The literal translation means "cinnabar field" or "red field" but a looser translation means "elixir field" or "magic field."

More specifically, it refers to the physical center of gravity located in the abdomen three finger-widths below and two-finger widths behind the navel. In Chinese and Japanese tradition it is considered the seat of one's internal energy or *ki.* A master of calligraphy, swordsmanship, tea ceremony, martial arts or comparable disciplines is held in the Japanese tradition to be "acting from the *hara.*" No matter how it is viewed, spiritually or physically, the core is what gives martial artists their "magic" strength.

In more scientific terms the *Hara* is a concentration of muscles known as the core muscles or stabilizer muscles. The optimal development of the core muscles is essential in the stabilization of the spine and the body in movement. The specific muscles include the transverse abdominus, rectus abdominus and the internal and external obliques, collectively known as the abdominals or the abs, the multifidus, quadratus lumborum and the erector spinae of the lower back and the pelvic floor muscles. The body is much like a chain with the links starting from the foot and running through the ankle, calf, knee, thigh and hip to the pelvis and spine and, thus, moving one part of the body would affect the other parts of the body. This chain is known as the kinetic chain and all the different parts come together in the core.

A weakness or instability, or any other problem, in one area could thus cause injury or pain in another area of the chain. If all of these muscles are strong and working in the correct order, a martial artist will have a solid base for movement and the ability to absorb the impact of direct hits to the body. A strong core makes all forms of movement more effective and improves posture, balance and athletic performance. It also reduces the risk of injury and increases strength and agility.

Of major importance to a karateka is that the correct use of the core allows for the transmission of forces from the lower body to the upper body or vice versa. In effect, this means that each strike has the strength and force of the entire body behind it. Another key feature of a well-developed core is that it assists in making movements more explosive. The core assists in every facet of combat and allows for stronger, quicker and more forceful strikes and kicks, the lifting and throwing of an opponent without inflicting personal injury, the quick and efficient twists making throwing an opponent over the hip easier and more efficient, the support of an opponent's weight, and the ability to twist and manipulate the opponent while ground fighting.

FREQUENCY AND INTENSITY OF ABDOMINAL WORKOUTS

Core training should be an integral part of a karateka's training cycle and form an essential part of the warm up and training. For persons who have no experience in strengthening their core, they would need slow and controlled movements conducted in a stable environment. The main objective, at an early stage of core conditioning, is to eliminate weaknesses and to become familiar with the basic abdominal exercises, focusing specifically on the muscles that need extra conditioning. The next stage, a more advanced level of core conditioning, is to intensify the training and work on multiple planes, meaning that exercises will be performed in the various planes of the body using combinations of different core muscles. At the optimal level of core development the goal is to maintain the acquired strength through training two to three times per week and, if the intention is to develop an exceptionally strong core, then training can be increased to five days a week. Finally, when training the core, a combination of strength training (short but heavy sets) and endurance training (lighter but more repetitions) must be applied.

BEGINNER WORKOUTS

Beginners start by doing two to three sets of ten to fifteen repetitions per set and gradually build up to twenty to thirty repetitions.

Basic Supported Crunch

1. Lie face up with your legs resting on a ball. This will support the lower back.
2. Lift your head and shoulders up off the ground with your hands resting on knees.
3. Slowly come up into a crunch position, sliding your hands over your knees and then slowly go back into the starting position.

Basic supported crunch using an exercise ball.

Lower Back Extensions

1. Lie face down with your hips resting on a ball and your elbows on the ground.

2. Keep your feet together and slowly lift your legs to straighten your body and return to start position.

Do not hyperextend and do not use momentum to flick your legs up. Do this movement in a slow and controlled fashion.

Lower back extensions with the assistance of an exercise ball.

Oblique Crunch

1. Lie face up with your left hand on the floor, right hand on the head, right leg pulled up and bent with the left leg crossed over the right.

2. Perform crunch with right elbow touching left knee.

3. Change position of hands and legs and repeat.

When performing oblique crunches ensure that the legs do not move.

Leg Extensions

1. Lie on a bench with your legs bent 90 degrees, and your back flat. Support your body by gripping the handles/side of bench.

2. Focus on keeping your back flat, then extend your legs and bring your back to 90 degrees.

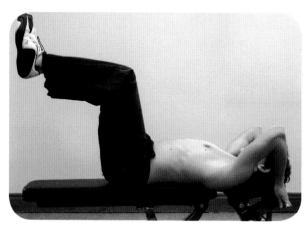 

Leg extensions may be performed in a dojo with the assistance of another karateka where a bench is not available.

INTERMEDIATE LEVEL WORKOUTS

Once you find that the basic movements have become easy to do, you can move on to exercises that are more challenging. They are done in three to four sets of fifteen to twenty-five repetitions.

Seated Russian Twists

1. From the seated position, suspend your feet off the ground.

2. While holding a medicine ball, rotate your shoulders side-to-side, touching the ball to the ground.

Keep your feet off the floor throughout the entire exercise.

When performing seated Russian twists the legs must not move.

Vertical Crunch

1. Lie face up on floor with your legs straight up.

2. Contract your abs and reach out towards your feet with your hands, attempting to touch them.

3. Keep your legs in a fixed position and imagine bringing your belly towards your spine at the top of the position.

4. Lower back into the starting position and repeat.

Weights can also be added to vertical crunch.

The neck must not change angle to the body when performing vertical crunches.

The vertical crunch exercise enhanced with a weight.

Bridging

1. Lie on your stomach, resting your upper body on your elbows.

2. Lift your hips up and hold the position with your body in a straight line, resting on your elbows and toes.

3. Hold this position for twenty to thirty seconds and repeat three times.

Work up to holding the position for one to two minutes.

It is important that the top of the buttocks lift slightly higher than the shoulders when bridging.

Side Bridging

This can be done in the same manner as normal bridging, only on the side, resting on one elbow and keeping both legs together.

*The legs and torso must form a very slight inverted V,
with the apex at the hips, when performing side bridging.*

MORE ADVANCED AND KARATE SPECIFIC EXERCISES:

These exercises are done in three sets with shorter repetitions of eight to ten, once sufficient strength has been gained increase the level of repetitions.

Seated leg Extensions

1. Sit on a bench with your legs up, supporting your upper body by holding onto the side of the bench, and keeping your back straight.

2. In one movement, extend your legs forward and bend your arms to lower your upper body.

3. Return to the upright position and repeat.

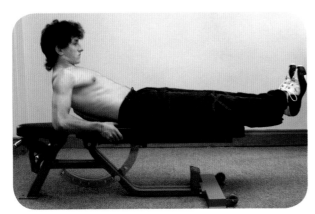 

The legs must not touch the bench or the ground when performing seated leg extensions.

Medicine Ball Push-Up

1. Put both of your hands on a medicine ball with your body straight, in a push-up position.

2. Bend your arms and let your chest touch the ball and push back up again.

Keep your body straight throughout the entire movement.

The key to medicine ball push-ups is keeping one's balance.

Bicycle Crunch

1. Lie face up on a mat with your fingers behind your ears.

2. Bring your knees in and lift your shoulders up off the ground.

3. Straighten your left leg out while simultaneously turning your body to the right, bringing your left elbow towards your right knee.

4. Switch sides, bringing your right elbow towards your left knee.

5. Continue alternating sides in a "pedalling" motion.

Ball Back Extensions

1. Lie face down with your hips and stomach on the ball, keeping balanced with your feet together on the floor.

2. Place your hands under your chin, next to your head.

3. Relax to slump down over the ball, and then squeeze your lower back to lift your chest off of the ball.

4. Raise up until your body is straight, but not hyperextended. Lower down and repeat.

Ball back extensions require much concentration to maintain balance.

Ball Transfer

1. Begin by lying on your back with your arms and legs straight up while holding the ball straight up over your body.

2. Take the ball in your hands and lower your arms and legs down towards the floor.

3. Bring your arms and legs back up and take the ball between your feet, squeezing them to keep the ball in place and lower your arms and legs down towards the floor.

4. Continue this movement by passing the ball between your hands and feet with extensions in between.

Ball transfer requires concentration and practice.

Hanging Leg Lifts

Hanging leg lifts can be done with bent legs or straight legs depending on the level of personal strength.

1. Start by holding onto handlebars and hanging in a vertical position.

2. Bend your knees and pull them up towards your chest, then back down again.

3. For a straight leg lift you will keep your legs straight and bring your body into a 90-degree angle before taking your legs back down again.

Hanging leg lifts can be done with bent legs or straight legs depending on the level of personal strength.

CONDITIONING TO PREVENT INTRINSIC INJURIES

Most karateka suffer from a variety of injuries during their active careers and even long after retirement they may continue to live in pain.

There are two main sources of injuries sustained during the practicing of karate, namely extrinsic (from outside the body) and intrinsic (from within the body). Examples of extrinsic factors would be trauma (for example, injuries caused by being punched) or training errors (e.g. lack of warm up, increasing training load too quickly or a change in surface or equipment used). Intrinsic factors internally affect an individual's body, and can be altered to reduce the chance of injury, and can usually improve performance.

In general, body types can be divided into two groups: flexible/ hyper mobile types that lean towards weakness, and inflexible types that may be strong or weak but tend to be stiff. There are those people who lie in the middle of this continuum of body type who are neither extreme.

For those who are very flexible, joint problems due to a lack of control and support of the joint structures are the most likely injuries. Examples of these include neck and back (vertebral joint) strain, strain of ligaments in the limbs (for example, knee and ankle) and chronic tendonitis due to continual stress on the tendon in an attempt to control excessive movement at the joint. These people may also suffer from spasms of the global (big moving) muscles as they attempt to compensate for the lack of strength in the small stabilizing muscles.

For those who are inflexible, stability at the joint tends to be less of a problem than it is for their more mobile counterparts. These people struggle with muscle tears and strains due to a lack of flexibility (or give) in their muscle and tendon tissue. Their joints are well-protected by their generally "tighter structures" but their muscles cannot always handle the flexibility demands of some of the required movements (for example, kicks and squats).

If a karateka is flexible (and therefore most likely weaker in the stabilizing muscles), the karateka probably needs exercises that address stability. The core muscles are the muscles that need to be developed. Classes for Pilates/ core exercises are widely available. Teaching and supervision by a qualified physiotherapist, Pilates instructor, biokineticist, or personal trainer, familiar with the *correct* methods of teaching these exercises, is imperative, at least initially, after which the karateka could continue to practice the principles learned and apply them during karate training sessions.

For those karateka who are inflexible, stretching is the key to injury prevention—yoga classes are an example of a group "cross training" exercise that would be beneficial to these karateka.

For karateka of all body types, posture during daily life and sport is key. Correct posture and postural habits naturally enhance core stability and reduce inflexibility. So postural retraining and awareness is something everyone should work on as a basic necessity to a healthy musculo-skeletal system.

CONDITIONING TO PREVENT EXTRINSIC INJURIES

Karate, particularly in the kumite aspects of training, can be very physical and the chance of being kicked or punched with sufficient force to cause pain or injury is high. Only once a karateka has actually been punched in the face, cracked a rib or been seriously injured will they really understand the need to condition their bodies to these extrinsic injuries in a gradual manner. The following are typical extrinsic body conditioning exercises.

Forearm and Inside Arm Conditioning

As the arms are the primary defense against attack they tend to take a lot of punishment. The arm, as pointed out in Chapter 12, "Body Hard Points," has some hard points and these can be made even harder through conditioning. The softer parts of the arm also need to be conditioned and through conditioning exercises karateka will soon find the hardest and softest parts of their arms. Karateka can, in controlled situations, condition their arms by using a wooden dummy or by standing face to face with another karateka and striking their arms against each other in a predetermined pattern and timing.

*Inside forearm
conditioning—step 1.*

*Inside forearm
conditioning—step 2.*

*Inside and outside forearm
conditioning—step 1.*

*Inside and outside forearm
conditioning—step 2.*

*Inside and outside forearm
conditioning—step 3.*

*Inside and outside forearm
conditioning—step 4.
Repeat series with left arm.*

Hand and Wrist Conditioning

Repetitive strong punches to a heavy punching bag or *makiwara* not only help develop speed and accuracy of these punches but the will also ensure that the karateka stikes the target with the fist closed correctly and the wrist in the lock position. Over time and with regular workouts the karateka will toughen the hands, callous the knuckles and strengthen the wrist.

The karateka can also work all the other strikes, listed in Chapter 5, "*Strikes and Kicks*," into these training aids to help develop the strength required for these blows.

Another training technique is for two karateka to face each other and strike their wrists together then clasp each other's wrists and then pull down on each other's wrists. This conditioning technique not only strengthens the wrist but also teaches karateka to work within their bodies' optimal postures. When pulling down, the karateka who keeps their arm tucked in will pull the other karateka off balance.

Wrist conditioning—step 1.

Wrist conditioning—step 2.

Wrist conditioning—step 3.

Leg and Feet Conditioning

In much the same way that hands and wrist are conditioned legs can be conditioned by bag work and, at a more advanced level, against harder objects. Never use the top of the foot against hard objects as the top of the foot is relatively weak.

Abdomen Conditioning

The abdomen is a very vulnerable part of the torso and has a number of pressure points, including the solar plexus, the lower rib cage and the zyphoid process, which can cause some serious discomfort when struck. It is important that karateka gradually improve their abdomen's strength until they can withstand a very solid blow. To do this karateka must practice being hit in the abdomen—not just in the center, but all over the abdomen. The strength of the strikes should be increased as the karateka's abdomen becomes stronger. While experimenting with this conditioning, karateka will find that it is the locations around the center of the abdomen that are most vulnerable and that they should make use of this knowledge when fighting.

Another exercise for conditioning both the arm and the abdomen is when two karateka face each other. The first karateka punches the other with the right hand with the objective of hitting the second karateka in the stomach. The second karateka tries to block the first karateka's punch with a left hand *uchi uke*, which the second karateka follows up with a right hand *uchi-uke* and then a *gedan-uke* using the left hand *gedan-uke*. The second karteka then tries to punch the first karateka in the stomach and the first karateka uses the same series of blocks to stop this punch. As the karateka become familiar with this sequence they can speed up the process.

Arm and abdomen conditioning—step 1.

Arm and abdomen conditioning—step 2.

Arm and abdomen conditioning—step 3.

Arm and abdomen conditioning—step 4.

Tai sabaki *in action.*

CHAPTER 18

IMPROVING YOUR FIGHTING SKILLS

ENVIRONMENTAL AWARENESS

For karateka, there are a number of different environments in which fighting may take place: routine training in a club, competitive fighting in a tournament or, in the worst-case scenario, a self-defense situation where the outcome of a fight means life or death. There are many different karate associations, each with their own rules, so even the environment from one competition to another may vary significantly. Each of these environments has its own requirements and, even in the case of self-defense fighting, its own set of rules.

A karateka should be able to adapt to these environments with ease. However, this is easier said than done. Standard karate training such as doing kata, *ippon* kumite, *jiyu* kumite and endless repetition is absolutely vital and no karateka will ever become an effective fighter without this training. However, specialized kumite training, environment-specific training and knowledge of the environment, including rules, will make all the difference between winning and losing.

Fitness, strength, speed, accuracy and knowledge of the body's pressure and hard points are vital to all fighting environments but these too can be honed to meet the specific requirements of a specific environment. Understanding of the environment is vital. Remember that kumite is just like a game of chess that is played at very high speed. A game of chess cannot be played unless the rules are known, and a game of chess can't be won unless a large number of tactics are known. To win a fight, a karateka needs to know the rules and needs as many tactics at their disposal as possible.

KNOWLEDGE OF THE RULES

When performing *jiyu* kumite in a class it is vital that karateka know the parameters under which they are fighting. Some pertinent questions to address include whether or not the kumite is full contact or light sparring, and if takedowns are permitted. This knowledge will prevent injuries and, by fighting within these parameters, the karateka is preparing to fight according to the rules of the given situation.

Competition kumite has plenty of rules. Knowing how to score points means that a karateka can focus on attacks that will win points and not cause a disqualification. Knowing the duration of a bout means that the fighter can pace themselves and their scoring. Understanding the terminology, hand signals and positioning ensures that the karateka can fight with focus and confidence. A good sensei will thoroughly explain the competition rules before students participate.

Believe it or not, street fighting does have rules. Most countries will prosecute an individual if they use excessive force when defending themselves. For example, if an individual is jabbed with a finger by an "attacker" who is simply using that finger to rudely make a point (which is seen as assault by many countries), and the "victim" overreacts by breaking the attacker's arm, it is the arm-breaking participant who will end up in the most trouble in the eyes of the law. Similarly if a man is slapped in the face by a woman and responds by knocking the woman out with a powerful punch, it is the man who will be in more trouble before the law. Karateka must beware of using excessive force should they ever be attacked.

A GOOD ARSENAL OF TRICKS

To win any fight, a karateka must be able to overcome an opponent's defense. In *jiyu* kumite and competition kumite opponents are prepared for attack and so are highly alert and ready to defend. The winning karateka is the one who is best able to overcome the other's defenses, and to do this you need a good arsenal of tactics. These include:

- Being able to perform a sequence of strikes and kicks one after the other, very quickly, without loosing focus, balance, strength and accuracy. Thus, when launching an attack, the opponent is completely overwhelmed and their defense falls apart. Karateka should have at least three or four combinations well rehearsed and thus, with sufficient muscle memory, be able to put the sequences into effect without thinking.

- Being able to quickly change fighting stance.

Changing the fighting stance.

- Learn to fight with either foot and with either hand. If one arm is weaker and less accurate than the other practice with the weak arm until it is able to perform as well as the strong arm. An opponent who is only able to fight with one footing will find themselves at a distinct disadvantage when suddenly attacked from a different position.

- Being able to close the distance with an opponent very quickly. This requires very quick footwork and the ability to judge distance extremely well. Practice against a punching bag or *makiwara* but, in closing the gap, never step in such a manner as to cross one leg over the other as this enables an opponent to perform an effective takedown.

Closing distance fast—step 1.

Closing distance fast—step 2.

Closing distance fast—step 3.

Do not cross your legs as this can cause a loss of balance if your opponent counter-attacks.

- Being able to deceive an opponent into believing a particular action is about to happen when in fact a very different action is put into effect. A good example is to perfect a *mawashi-geri* that starts off as a *mae-geri* but changes, just before being blocked, from a lunge into a roundhouse kick. This kick then evades the downward defense and goes around the downward blocking arm to impact on the side of the head or torso of the opponent.

- Being able to encourage an opponent to make an attack that can be controlled. For example, an attacker may place his hands low in a defensive stance thus luring an opponent into thinking that a *jodan zuki* would be effective. The attacker is thus expecting the *jodan zuki* and is able to block the punch effectively before counter striking.

| *Good stance with hands kept intentionally low to lure an attack.* | *Poor movement—the head is too far forward and the hands have been dropped as the body moves.* | *Bad fighting stance—the feet are too far apart making it easy for an opponent to sweep the front foot.* |

- Being able to launch an attack without any telltale signs. Many karateka needlessly telegraph their intentions with a grimace, tensed bodies, clenched fist or cocked arm before attacking. These bad habits must be eradicated as an experienced opponent will read these signs and effectively defend an attack or launch a pre-emptive strike.

- Being able to defend effectively. Karateka must be able to keep their defense up at all times including when launching an attack. The position of arms and hands must always be maintained in a position that provides optimum defence.

- A good fighting stance will ensure that sweeps and takedowns will be difficult for an opponent to implement.

- Blocking within the body's boundaries is vital to maintaining good balance and thus a position from which to launch a counter-strike.

- Being able to move the entire body away from an opponent's strike without losing balance. This is known as *tai sabaki*. This movement must be very quick and happen without losing balance, thus ensuring that a quick counter-attack can be put into effect.

- Being able to react toward an opponent's attack rather than away from the opponent's attack. This takes much training and practice but ensures that the opponent is always kept off balance.

Tai sabaki *in action. Note that the defender, although moving away from the attacker's strike, properly distances himself from the attacker, and is able to counter-attack.*

BUILDING STRENGTH AND SPEED

When it comes to striking, whether with fist, elbow, knee or foot, speed is strength. The faster the strike the harder it will impact. Forced, tension-based strength tends to reduce the speed of a punch and, as mentioned previously, informs the opponent that a strike is imminent. The best strikes are those that are delivered with a relaxed speed. This may sound contradictory but the biokinetics of the matter show that a muscle that becomes tense slows down. One of the reasons that karateka do so many repetitive punches is that this builds muscle memory and makes it easier for the karateka to punch quickly. Punching with a continuously tensed arm and body is not only slower, but also very tiring. The tension in the strike should only happen moments before impact.

FITNESS AND ACCURACY

Three minutes may not sound like a long time when shopping or driving to work but in a fight, three minutes is a very long time. A fairly high level of fitness is required to be able to fight continuously for three minutes and any karateka who wishes to compete effectively must be able to fight well for four three-minute bouts with a minute's break in between each bout. This requires a high level of fitness. One way for a karateka to gauge his fitness level is to continuously punch and kick a heavy punching bag, with enough force to keep the punching bag swinging, for three minutes. If this can't be done, the karateka is wasting their time entering a competition.

Accuracy is closely related to fitness. As a fighter tires, so accuracy becomes more and more difficult until punches and kicks become so inaccurate that they are unable to score points. Thus, when training for a fight, it is necessary to be able to not just punch and kick that bag for three minutes but to do so accurately for three minutes.

FIGHTING EXERCISES FOR COMPETITIONS

The following excercises will increase your readiness to compete:

- Mark out the size of the competition dojo and move around the dojo, at first keeping an eye on the floor markings and then practice doing so without looking at the markings. This will ensure familiarity with the dojo size and help prevent accidental movement off the dojo while fighting.

- Practice accurate striking and kicking. Make use of training aids such as jab pads, a punching bag with marked target points and a speed ball.

- Train wearing all the kit required by the competition rules such as groin protectors, mouthguard, and so on. This will ensure that these items do not cause any discomfort or uncertainty when fighting.

FIGHTING EXERCISES FOR SELF-DEFENSE

Here are three dojo training techniques for self-defense kumite:

- Circle of fear—the students stand in a large open circle facing inwards. Two karateka, one on the inside and one on the outside of the circle, walk around the circle together. On a sharp instruction from the sensei they attack the student who stands between them. The other karateka move away and allow the sparring to continue for a few seconds.

- Triangle of fear—a student stands in the middle of three other students who each have a number. The sensei shouts the number of one of the students on the outside who then attacks the student on the inside. The sensei may activate more than one attacker at a time.

- Three-way—three students are confined to an area and are instructed to perform *jiyu* kumite with each other at the same time.

- Double trouble—a student stands between two other students. The instructor shouts numbers and the student in the middle must attack the person on the left if an odd number is called and attack the student on the right if an even number is called.

Double trouble in action. In practice this exercise requires skill in judging distance and excellent foot work to be able to move from one position to another very quickly.

Bearing in mind that self-defense is unlikely to occur in the perfect environment of a dojo, there are a number of techniques that can be used to simulate difficult environments:
- Perform kata while blindfolded to improve balance and positioning.
- Practice *jiyu* kumite with hands tied behind the back to strengthen leg techniques and improve balance.
- Perform *yakusoko* kumite with one eye blindfolded to improve distance judgement.
- Perform kata on the beach while being struck by waves.
- Practice punches, kicks and blocks while balancing on a small object or while balancing on one leg.
- Practice punches, kicks and blocks while sitting in a car, on the floor or on a flight of stairs.
- Practice blocking and counter-striking against an opponent armed with, at first, a toy edged weapon. Once sufficient confidence has been gained, practice against an opponent armed with a real edged weapon.
- Practice blocking and counter-striking against an opponent armed with a blunt weapon.

The clinch.

CHAPTER 19

KARATE AND MIXED MARTIAL ARTS

HOW WOULD A KARATEKA PERFORM IN AN MMA EVENT?

An average karateka, who trains eight hours a week, would be demolished in a few seconds in a professional MMA event. To begin with, this is a stupid question, like asking: how would a person who jogs three times a week compete in an Olympic marathon event? You don't need to be a rocket scientist to know the answer. Professional MMA entrants are super-fit, well-conditioned to taking extreme punishment to their bodies and have a range of fighting skills honed to a particular fighting environment and set of rules. The average black belt karateka practices mostly non-contact fighting with its own set of rules. By the same token, an MMA fighter would be quickly disqualified from, say, a WKF kumite event.

HOW WOULD AN MMA FIGHTER WITH KARATE TRAINING FARE IN AN MMA EVENT?

This is a slightly more intelligent question and the answer would be: All things being constant, the karateka would do just as well as any other trained martial artists. However, the reality of MMA events is that the fighters have a large amount of cross-training. Karate, in its basic form, only offers techniques that would be used in one of three main phases of a typical MMA fight, namely "stand up." When it comes to "clinch" and "ground" fighting, then the MMA fighter will draw on other styles of martial arts such as wrestling or judo for the clinch and Brazilian jiu-jitsu for the ground fighting.

FOR SELF-DEFENSE, WHICH IS BEST: MMA OR KARATE?

At a basic level, both are very good for self-defense. Having some fighting ability is far better than having no fighting ability. However, MMA does break one of the key rules of self-defense and that is to never allow yourself to be contained by an attacker. By clinching and particularly by going to the ground, the defender is very vulnerable to a second or third attacker, and also prevented from exercising the very best form of self-defense: getting out of the danger area. In the case of law enforcement or military personnel the primary weapon of the defender will not be hands and feet but a gun, club or knife and these cannot be drawn when one is in a clinch or on the ground.

An example of standup fighting.

Ground fighting in progress.

At an advanced level, karate is far better. A karateka's natural instinct is to keep the attacker at a distance where evasion can take place or the primary weapon can be drawn. Remember, karate has been developed for self-defense over thousands of years by martial artists who have dedicated their life to finding the optimal way for dealing with all possible forms of attack excluding those of ranged weapons. To the layman, watching a karate class perform repetitive actions and kata, this may seem ridiculous. However, in reality, the kata that are performed with such repetition are in fact pre-planned defensive actions against attacks from edged and blunt weapons as well as from fists. A karateka who understands the *bunkai* of these kata will easily show you how many of the techniques used by reality-based fighting arts are, in fact, applications of kata.

At an even more advanced level, karateka learn to use the basic blocks, strikes and stances to evade a clinch, and take an attacker to the ground without falling to the ground themselves. At this advanced level of karate, many of the kata can be interpreted and applied as techniques that are used by an equally advanced level of judo or jiu jitsu. In other words, at advanced levels of karate, judu, aikido, tae kwon do and kung fu and many other martial arts, the techniques applied to defend against a specific attack are the same or very similar. The only difference between these styles is the training path that has been followed to get to that advanced level of application.

HOW CAN KARATE ENHANCE A MIXED MARTIAL ARTIST'S SKILLS?

Any MMA practitioner who has trained extensively in one of the traditional martial arts will find becoming an MMA fighter easier than somebody who begins their martial arts career with MMA. Thus, it will be relatively easy for a karateka to become a mixed martial artist.

A mixed martial artist with a karate base will also find it relatively easy to learn the clinching and ground fighting techniques as most of the traditional martial arts, no matter what their focus, work on the same fundamentals as karate. Most stand up and even some clinch styles use similar stances, strikes, kicks and movements. The economy of movement, speed, accuracy, balance, focus, pressure points and hard points that a karateka has learned will also enhance the karateka's fighting skill as a mixed martial artist.

Assuming that the mixed martial artist has their key martial arts training in a style other than the stand up arts such as Muay Thai, Tae Kwon Do, Kick Boxing, or Savat, there is an enormous amount that an MMA fighter can learn from karate and in most cases the professionals do draw their stand up fighting skills from karate or one of the other styles mentioned above.

ARE THERE DISADVANTAGES TO BASING MMA ON KARATE?

Karate training does not involve much contact and karateka will find themselves at a disadvantage when switching to the very physical MMA which has a heavy impact on the body. Karateka who have trained in the full-contact aspect of karate will be at less of a disadvantage. If a karateka is planning to participate in MMA events, it is essential that they be very fit before entering a competition and that they work on their body conditioning. The higher the level of fitness, the less likely the karateka will be injured and the quicker the karateka will recover from any injuries sustained.

Martial artists who base their MMA fighting on judo or wrestling will have very strong hands as a consequence of the grappling and clinching and will also be comfortable with having their opponent's blood, sweat and tears splashed and ground into their own bodies. This takes some getting used to for the average karateka.

Mixed martial artists wear shorts and not a gi. This is not a serious matter and karateka will soon feel at home in the new outfit. However, karateka, who for years have fought in competitions with thick, padded mitts will immediately notice the difference in impact when being hit by a lightly gloved, knuckled fist. MMA does not allow shin protectors either and so karateka will have to toughen up their legs. A *mawashi-geri*, a great point-scorer in karate, can be a big disadvantage in MMA if applied incorrectly. As pointed out in Chapter 12, "Body Hard Points," the foot is fairly delicate and a skilled MMA fighter will relish the opportunity to smash his forearm into the foot at the end of *mawashi-geri* kick. This will disable the kicker.

WHAT ARE THE ADVANTAGES OF BASING MMA ON KARATE?

Karate provides one of the best arsenals of skills for stand up fighting. Karate kicks, strikes and blocks are extremely powerful and, as has been seen in many MMA events, these can be enough to win a fight, usually by knockout. If a karateka makes use of the arsenal of tactics listed in the previous chapter and modifies them for the rules and conditions of MMA, a karateka will have one of the three aspects of an MMA fight—stand up fighting—wrapped up.

The solidity of karate stances and movements means that a karateka has a distinct advantage in the clinching aspects of a fight against a martial artist whose skills lie entirely in ground fighting. Even against clinch specialists such as *judoka* and wrestlers, a karateka, thanks to their well-trained *hara*, will be able to offer some effective resistance, particularly in evading a clinch and escaping from an applied clinch. Once out of the clinch, the karateka is again on home territory and at an advantage.

The economy of movement, coordinated breathing and intense focus taught by many of the Eastern martial arts, such as karate, ensures that a karateka also has the basics on which to build fight stamina.

Karateka who have fought in kumite events can also draw on their experience with movement, closing with an opponent, reading an opponent's body language and all the other similarities that kumite shares with a MMA fight.

WHAT IS THE FUNDAMENTAL DIFFERENCE BETWEEN KARATE AND MMA?

One of the five maxims, the *dojo kun*, of karate is not to seek aggression whereas MMA is fundamentally an aggressive sport. A substantial number of karateka will go through their whole karate career without ever participating in any kumite events, let alone any full contact karate. A large number of relatively new styles of karate guarantee their students that there is no hard contact in their class and that their karate is non-competitive. Many karateka, contrary to the character of traditional karate spirit, have little interest in kumite and derive all their pleasure from kata. In short, many people enjoy doing karate because it is not overtly aggressive but is still physical. MMA is all about aggression.

MMA is also highly commercial, drawing crowds as big as those of professional boxing. Many of the rules that govern MMA have been introduced, in the past few years, to make the sport more commercially viable. Karate on the other hand has little commercial value with world championship events drawing relatively small crowds of spectators.

Karate is, perhaps, the more difficult to master as it requires more character, sincerity, effort, etiquette and self-control to perform. It is good for the body, mind and soul.

Few attacks occur unaccompanied by the use of a weapon.

CHAPTER 20

KARATE AND SELF-DEFENSE

VIOLENCE SHOULD BE A LAST RESORT

Most karate books have a chapter titled "self-defense" and then go to great lengths showing you a series of moves, none of which have any links to karate techniques, that can be used when defending oneself. This is ridiculous as every move that has been taught in karate may be used in self-defense. In fact karate techniques are the sum of thousands of years of knowledge that has been accumulated by martial artists who actually fought in wars, in self-defense and in aggression, and these techniques have been been honed to a fine fighting edge. Why now go and create some new techniques when karate has all the tools you need for fighting? Many people argue that karate is impractical and not effective in the real world. Try telling this to the warriors who have used karate over the centuries or the founders of reality based fighting techniques who base their methods on the ancient martial arts such as karate. Karate kata are self defense in action and they are in fact exercises that can save your life.

Having said this, it does not matter how well trained you are, how fit, strong or quick you may be or even if you have a weapon, unless you are ready for an attack, the attacker will always have a huge advantage—surprise. Surprise is the single best weapon in combat. Criminals do not, as the movies suggest, jump in front of you and tell you what they are going to do to you. They attack from behind or when you are sitting in a car or searching for your keys in your hand bag, or when you are asleep, or when you are walking on crutches—basically any time you are unprepared and in no position to fight. Criminals, like wild animals, prey on the weak and defenseless as this greatly reduces their risk of injury or being caught. If you make sure that you're less vulnerable than those around you, you will never be attacked unless the attacker has a personal vendetta against you.

An experienced karateka will tell you that there is always somebody who can, for whatever reason, beat you in combat. Nobody ever wins every fight and you only have to lose one real life fight to lose your life. An experienced karateka will also tell you to *never* underestimate an opponent; in real life this can be fatal. You may be a brilliant karateka but when you come up against a hardened criminal who has no problem with hurting you or even killing you, you are at a disadvantage. It was for these very reasons that Tode Sakugawa said, in his five maxims of karate, "Violence should be a last resort." You only fight if there is no other choice, if every other possibility has been exhausted.

AWARENESS—YOUR FIRST LINE OF DEFENSE

The first line of self-defense is, quite simply, being aware of your environment. If you are careful, you will never have to fight. If you are aware of potential danger you can take the necessary precautions to prevent the danger from harming you. These precautions can be as simple as locking your car door, or more advanced, such as installing an alarm system. Awareness, in this sense, is a very broad term as it covers knowledge of geography, events, timing, behavior, local knowledge, and body language.

Geographical awareness is knowing which areas are danger hot-spots. These areas can be large, such as a war zone or a suburb, or small, such as a dark parking lot late at night, a traffic intersection that has a high incidence of high-jackings, or even a nightclub with a violent history. Whenever possible avoid these areas, or, if you have no choice, heighten your sense of awareness and make yourself less vulnerable.

Event awareness includes protest marches, rioting, or a sporting event or political rally with potentially violent spectators. Watch the news and avoid these events. If they can't be avoided, be aware and be prepared.

Timing awareness covers periods of time when you are vulnerable to attack such as getting into/out of a motor vehicle or searching for keys when arriving home late at night. Limit your vulnerability by being aware of these times and try to perform these functions in a secure environment.

Behavioral awareness involves taking note of any personal behavior that may place you in a dangerous situation. Typical examples would be: reacting to road rage, picking up hitchhikers, or performing the same behavior pattern with such regularity that it makes you an easy target for criminals. Drawing large amounts of cash from the same bank every day at the same time allows the criminal to plan an effective attack and take you by surprise. Think before you react, think before you act and act in an unpredictable manner.

A large number of attacks take place in areas that are frequented by the victim. The victim has, through regular behavior, made themselves vulnerable. However, it is not always easy to change behavior, as work, family, and other commitments may not be flexible. In this case local knowledge is important and being aware of unusual activities, cars, people, or environmental differences, such as arriving home and noticing that a light you remember switching off is now on, can be indicators of danger. Know your environment and when something appears out of place try to determine if it can result in a dangerous situation before placing yourself in the situation. If you suspect danger, call the police.

Understanding people's body language can make all the difference between getting into a fight or not, and after years of karate training you should be able to identify, through body language, when an individual is aggressive, volatile, and/or looking for trouble. The years of facing off against other karateka who, on the dojo floor, are tense, reactionary and in fighting mode makes it easy to identify people who exhibit the same or similar tendencies on the street. In fact, you should be able to walk through a shopping center or enter a nightclub and almost instantly be able to identify persons who are overtly looking for trouble. Stay away from these people. Add the evaluation of body language to your awareness checklist and you may find that you can go through your entire life without ever having to physically defend yourself.

The driver of the car is clearly not concentrating on her surroundings. She is talking on her cell phone with her window down and the hand holding the phone is closest to the window. Put these together and she becomes an easy target for a snatch and grab.

The driver is encouraging an attack by leaving her possessions within easy reach of potential robbers. Her purse is on the seat next to her rather than on the floor, her window is down and her cell phone has been left on dashboard.

The driver is again not concentrating—she is talking on her cell phone, and is getting out of her car at the same time. This lack of focus makes her an easy target for a carjacking. In addition, the warning signs that she is in a rough neighborhood are evident—broken windows, razorwire, and so on.

FIVE POINT SELF-DEFENSE PLAN

A question commonly asked by karate students is "How effective is karate for self defense?" The answer is: Very good, but fighting is your absolute last resort. Karateka should understand there are options other than fighting available to them and these are best to get themselves out of potentially violent situations.

1. Avoidance

As mentioned earlier in this chapter, awareness is your single best defense, which can help you to avoid being attacked. Train yourself to be aware by:

- Watching people's movements and expressions.
- Memorize the cars that park in your street.
- Obtain police statistics on crime hotspots in your hometown.
- Ensure that your home has adequate security, particularly at the point of entry and exit.
- Memorize vital telephone numbers such as family and emergency services.
- Identify behavioral patterns that your family practices that make you vulnerable and change these practices.
- Scan your environment before getting out of a car, unlocking your front door, drawing money from an Automatic Teller Machine, and so on.
- Only allowing close friends and family to be within touching distance and professional contacts should be kept at arm's length. Don't allow people who you may feel to be a threat closer than twenty-one feet or seven meters. If professional contacts or threats come closer than the prescribed distances then you must be ready to fight.

2. Escape

Identify scenarios in which you are most likely to be attacked and determine in advance how you will react to them. For example, your job entails you carrying large amounts of cash from your office to the bank.

To minimize the chance of attack do the transfers at irregular intervals. Carry the cash in a variety of different packages. Follow different routes to the bank. Don't follow any procedure that is likely to warn potential criminals of your intention to carry the cash such as asking a staff member to accompany you to your car only when you are carrying the cash.

If you are attacked while carrying the cash think of the quickest way to hand the cash to the criminals without causing them to panic or overreact. Don't make eye contact with the criminals.

This kind of planning that will ensure that you escape being victimized, or, in the event of an attack, escape without injury.

3. Use the Environment

If possible, find a weapon of your own as quickly as possible. A rock, a broken bottle, a pen or even a bunch of keys will all come in handy and perhaps discourage your attacker from further violence. Just remember that if you draw a weapon you must be prepared to use it. Shout for help or cause a disturbance if there are people near by. If you feel that your life is sufficiently under threat do the unexpected but slightly less risky action of jumping into a river, running into the middle of a road, crashing your car, or any other activity that may help you escape.

4. Mobility

Ensure that you stay fit and healthy. Work on your distance perception, timing and accuracy to determine a safe distance between yourself and an attacker armed with an edged, impact, projectile or chemical weapon. When under attack always try to protect your mobility so that you can escape as soon as possible. Avoid being tied up or secured at almost all costs, particularly if you may be required to defend a loved one with you.

5. Fight

This is the last resort and is only worthwhile if your or a loved one's life is at stake.

FIGHTING

Karate training prepares you for fighting. The longer you have been doing karate the greater your muscle memory and the more likely you will enter a state of *mushin* when attacked. Bearing in mind that you will, in all likelihood, be attacked when you least expect it, it is this ability to react instantly with the right technique that will protect you and, quite possibly, save your life. Yasutsune Itosu, the father of modern karate, said that by knowing the five basic katas, the *Pinan* or *Heian* katas, the average man would be able to defend themselves effectively. The key word here is *knowing*. A karateka with a few months training will know the sequence of movements of these kata, but it will take constant, repetitive training, with much focus on improving balance, speed, and accuracy to ensure that body positioning, strikes and blocks become effective enough to defend oneself from a determined attacker. The very reason why karate is so repetitive is to build up muscle memory and to develop *mushin*.

Having said that, there are many instances where persons, with only rudimentary karate training such as policemen and soldiers, have successfully used the skills they have learned in a short karate course to defend themselves.

The world has changed substantially since the days of the old karate masters, there are new weapons, new environments, new threats and even new techniques. Styles such *Krav Maga* and *Systema* focus on these weapons (guns, grenades) and environments (motor vehicles, airplanes, airports) and have developed techniques to deal with them. Yet there is still an optimum way to strike and block, all developed by karate, and, of course, our bodies have not changed, and so the core, the *hara*, remains the center of all these styles.

Reality defense doesn't happen in a dojo environment but on a flight of stairs, in a tightly packed crowd, a dark alley or when you're using both hands to carry a heavy object. It is for this reason that karate training, at the more advanced levels, needs to be practiced in difficult environments. In *The Karate Kid*, the key character practiced his winning technique on a pole on the beach. This may look stupid, but if you can do this technique on a pole you can do this technique just about anywhere. It is well worth creating challenging environments in which to practice karate.

Chapter 18, "Improving Your Fighting Skills," deals extensively with techniques that help improve fighting skill and the ability to fight under adverse circumstances.

FENDING OFF WEAPONS

Very few physical attacks happen without the use of some form of weapon. The criminal wants to ensure that they have every advantage and so will certainly see to it that they are better armed than you are. Reality-based fighting styles identify five types of weapon frequently used in personal attacks, namely:

- Projectile weapons such as firearms, throwing knives, stones, or catapults.
- Edged weapons such as knives, broken bottles, scalpels, or screwdrivers.
- Impact weapons such as batons, baseball bats, or blackjacks.
- Chemical weapons such as pepper sprays or acids.
- Weapons of mass destruction such as Molotov cocktails, hand grenades, or pipe bombs.

In the case of projectile, chemical and mass destruction weapons, knowledge is your best defense. Instructors should take time out to understand these weapons, how long it takes for them to be applied, what is their range and how best to minimize their effect. Knowledge and understanding will always overcome fear and it is worthwhile developing some basic techniques to deal with these situations and passing them on to your students.

ADVANCED SELF-DEFENSE APPLICATION OF STANDARD KATA AND TECHNIQUES

Many kata, including the *Pinan/Heian* include techniques that are used to fend off attacks by edged and impact weapons and these kata even provide the techniques for disarming the attacker. It is important that instructors understand these *bunkai* and are able to show them to their students and include the training of these techniques in class.

Advanced Application of *Age-uke*

Application of **age-uke**.

Advanced Application of *Shuto-uke*

The *shuto-uke* is a block specifically used to disarm an opponent attacking with an edged weapon. The block is, in effect, a double strike, the first strike being on the ulna or radial nerve of the forearm of the attacker and the second strike being the median nerve of the attacker's arm. These two strikes will, with sufficient force, disable the attacker's arm and result in the edged weapon being dropped.

A traditional **shuto-uke** *move.*

Application of a **shuto-uke** *strike to the ulna or radial nerve.*

Application of a **shuto-uke** *strike on the median nerve.*

Advanced Application of Elements of *Pinan Shodan*

Pinan Shodan is one of the first kata a karateka will learn, but every move that is enacted is very effective in combat. The first two pictures show the move as it is performed in the kata. The last three pictures show the defender is striking the attacker's median nerve as the attacker tries to stab, the defender then pulls the attacker off balance and finally dislocates the attacker's shoulder joint.

The **Pinan Shodan** *technique.*

Application of **Pinan Shodan**.

Advanced Application of the Elements of *Pinan Sandan*

This is the final movement in *Pinan Sandan* and is a very effective double strike, one to the opponent's throat and the other to the solar plexus.

*A typical **Pinan Sandan** move.*

*Application of **Pinan Sandan** in self-defense.*

Advanced Application of elements of *Pinan Godan*

The first two moves in *Pinan Godan* are a block and an attack to the opponent's throat or chin.

*A typical **Pinan Godan** move.*

*Application of **Pinan Godan** in self-defense.*

ABOUT THE AUTHOR

Graeme John Lund was born in Johannesburg, South Africa in 1968, at a time when the turmoil of the government's apartheid policy resulted in widespread violence. Being from a middle class family he was seldom directly affected with the exception that, security, at home, on the road, or at school, was always an issue. Graeme's parents were fervently anti-apartheid and his father, in particular, often landed in hot water for his beliefs and for his frequent defense of individuals suffering under repression. His father's courage was re- markable and has had a profound effect on Graeme's life. It was at university that Graeme found that he enjoyed adrenalin-fueled sports. His weekends, and the odd weekday too, were spent rock-climbing, hiking, spear fishing, sky diving, bungee jumping, fencing, and scuba diving. In the early 1990's apartheid was dismantled but the violence within South Africa did not decline. It was during one such violent encounter that Graeme realized that he needed better knowledge and skill to deal with such situations. He joined a karate club and found that the martial arts weren't just good exercise but were very mentally challenging too. Competitive karate also provided the adrenalin that Graeme enjoyed. Graeme fell in love with karate and did every other martial course that he came across from bodyguarding to biokinetics. In 2007 Graeme suffered an injury to his shoulder which prevented him from active participation in karate classes and it was at this time that Graeme wrote *The Essential Karate Book*. Karate remains an important part of his life.